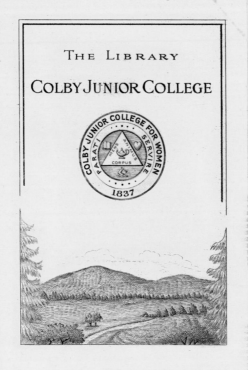

S0-BRB-483

GREAT PICTURES

of

EUROPE

FIG. 1. THE PENTECOST
By El Greco. *See p. 93*

GREAT PICTURES

of

EUROPE

By

THOMAS MUNRO

With 100
Illustrations

TUDOR PUBLISHING COMPANY
1934

FOREWORD

This is a short introduction to the appreciation of painting. It is written in the form of a guide-book to the principal art museums of Europe, and is therefore arranged, not chronologically, but according to the countries, cities, galleries and churches where important pictures are to be found. The order followed is that of a continuous trip, from England down through France and Spain, over to Italy and north through Austria and Germany. But each section of the book is independent in itself, and each museum is discussed separately. So the book can be read in any order of parts, and adapted to any itinerary.

In order to adapt it also for use in this country, or on the way to Europe, a large number of full-page illustrations have been given. Each of these is critically analyzed in some detail, while shorter comments are made on many other pictures not reproduced.

Extreme conciseness has been one of the principal aims throughout: not to mention all the pictures worth seeing if one had unlimited time, but to select from the countless thousands of pictures which clamor for one's attention in Europe a comparative few which should be seen without fail.

The hundred pictures reproduced, and the others mentioned, are not proposed as the best pictures in Europe, in any absolute sense. A list of that sort would be largely an expression of the author's personal preference, and it might well be restricted to the works of some ten or twenty supremely great artists. The standard of selection here has been not only quality but variety: to give a broadly representative list, including typical works not only of the greatest artists, but of many minor ones, each unique and interesting in his own way. Even among the hundred pictures reproduced and analyzed at length, are examples not only of the well-known European masters and schools, such as the Florentine and Dutch, but of the less familiar primitive and exotic types, such as ancient Roman, Byzantine, Chinese and Persian — all distinctive and important for a broad appreciation of art. The book will thus be useful, it is hoped, not only as a guide-book for travellers, but for students in this country, as a critical survey of the main types and traditions in the history of art.

Another aim in selection has been to suggest the particular strong points of each museum and city, in order to help the traveller decide in advance which places he would like to visit. At Vienna, for example, where Brueghel and Rubens are represented by many of their best works, a picture by each is reproduced and criticized; at Madrid, Velazquez and Goya are chosen for the same reason. In order to emphasize such distinctive, typical examples, occasional good pictures by the same men elsewhere are necessarily omitted, with no implication that they are inferior. What is said of a given artist somewhere in the book should be a hint to the traveller to watch out for occasional works by that man elsewhere, and also a hint as to what qualities are likely to be present in them.

The qualities emphasized throughout are those of pictorial form. There has been no attempt to provide entertaining anecdotes about the painters or their subjects, or poetic rhapsodies enjoyable in themselves as literature. In fact, an analysis of form is apt to be rather prosy reading in itself. It should be read only with frequent glances at the picture under discussion, so that the reader may see for himself each quality pointed out. Even then it requires effort at first, as learning a new language does. The enjoyment increases gradually, as one learns to grasp with ease what is said in the language of lines, colors, lights and shadows.

Try as one may to be objective, and to point out only what any reader with good eyesight and ordinary human feelings can experience, the individual viewpoint of the writer plays a part. Indeed, it is frankly expressed as such in these pages, along with other comments which are more purely visual and indisputable. To exclude it entirely would be useless as well as impossible. By far the greater part of what is said will, it is believed, be verifiable by the reader himself if he looks carefully at the picture under discussion. The rest is offered, not as a final statement of fact, but as a possible stimulus to each reader to see and feel for himself, and to compare the result with what he has read. To assist in that individual, independent picture-study, a questionnaire is given in the second part of the Introduction.

It remains for the author to express his thanks to those who have helped to make this book possible. My principal indebtedness in this regard is to the Barnes Foundation, which, during my association there, placed at my disposal invaluable opportunities for the study of painting in this country and in Europe; and especially to its president, Dr. A. C. Barnes, for suggestive criticism and for his own penetrating analyses of pictorial form. This is said, of course, with no desire to distribute responsibility for individual judgments expressed. A second acknowledgment is to Rutgers University and especially to the Dean of its College of Arts and Sciences, Dr. Walter T. Marvin, for his generous interest in facilitating my present work there in the teaching of aesthetics and art appreciation.

T. M.

CONTENTS

PAGE

List of Illustrations   xi

Introduction   xvii

1. Different Values in Painting
2. A Questionnaire for Picture-analysis
3. An Outline of the History of Painting

Chapter I. ENGLAND   1

The National Gallery. The Wallace Collection. The Millbank Branch of the National Gallery. The British Museum. Other Galleries in London.

Chapter II. FRANCE   41

The Louvre. The Luxembourg. Other Pictures in Paris. Outside of Paris.

Chapter III. SPAIN   87

Madrid: the Prado. Toledo and the Escorial.

PAGE

Chapter IV. ITALY   104

*Naples: the National Museum. Rome: the
Vatican and other Museums. Orvieto,
Assisi, Perugia and Arezzo: Churches and
Museums. Siena: Museum and Cathe-
dral. Florence: the Uffizi and Pitti; the
Academy; Churches and Palaces. Venice:
the Academy; the School of San Rocco;
the Basilica, and other Churches. Other
Towns in the North.*

Chapter V. AUSTRIA AND GERMANY   191

*Vienna: the Kunsthistorisches Museum; the
Albertina, Czernin and other Collections.
Munich: the Alte and Neue Pinako-
thek; the New State Gallery, and Other
Galleries. Dresden: the Gemäldegalerie,
Old and New Parts; Other Galleries.*

Chapter VI. BELGIUM AND HOLLAND   257

*Antwerp: the Museum of Fine Arts. Brus-
sels: the Old Museum. Bruges and Ghent.
Amsterdam: the Ryksmuseum. The
Hague: the Mauritshuis. Haarlem.*

Chapter VII. RUSSIA   276

*Leningrad: the Hermitage. Moscow: the
Museum of Modern Art.*

Index of Painters, with Dates   285

LIST OF ILLUSTRATIONS

FIGURE   PAGE

1. El Greco. THE PENTECOST. *Madrid*   *Frontispiece*

2. Uccello. THE ROUT OF SAN ROMANO. *London*   3

3. Titian. BACCHUS AND ARIADNE. *London*   5

4. Van Eyck. JOHN ARNOLFINI AND HIS WIFE. *London*   8

5. El Greco. THE AGONY IN THE GARDEN. *London*   10

6. Constable. THE HAYWAIN. *London*   12

7. Turner. ULYSSES DERIDING POLYPHEMUS. *London*   15

8. Fragonard. THE SWING. *London*   18

9. Seurat. BATHERS. *London*   20

10. Blake. SATAN SMITING JOB. *London*   22

11. Egyptian. MUSIC AND DANCING AT A BANQUET. *London*   26

12. Mu Ch'i. TIGER. *London*   28

13. Chinese, Ming Dynasty. THE EARTHLY PARADISE. *London*   30

14. Hokusai. RATS AND CAPSICUM PODS. *London*   32

xi

FIGURE   PAGE

15. Utamaro. A GIRL AND HER REFLECTION.
    London   34

16. Persian. THE MINISTERS OF HORMUZD PLEAD-
    ING FOR HIS SON. *London*   36

17. Indian (Mughal). SCENE FROM A ROMANCE.
    London   39

18. Leonardo da Vinci. MONA LISA. *Paris*   45

19. Giorgione. A CONCERT IN THE OPEN AIR.
    Paris   49

20. Titian. THE MAN WITH THE GLOVE. *Paris*   51

21. Mantegna. CALVARY. *Paris*   53

22. Lotto. ST. JEROME. *Paris*   55

23. Poussin. ORPHEUS AND EURYDICE. *Paris*   57

24. Claude Lorrain. CLEOPATRA DISEMBARKING
    AT TARSUS. *Paris*   59

25. Watteau. THE EMBARKATION FOR CYTHERA.
    Paris   61

26. Boucher. DIANA BATHING. *Paris*   63

27. Chardin. STILL LIFE. *Paris*   65

28. Ingres. ODALISQUE. *Paris*   68

29. Delacroix. ALGERIAN WOMEN. *Paris*   70

30. Monet. THE REGATTA AT ARGENTEUIL. *Paris*   72

31. Renoir. AT THE MOULIN DE LA GALETTE.
    Paris   75

32. Degas. THE STAR. *Paris*   77

FIGURE   PAGE

33. Matisse. ODALISQUE. *Paris*   84

34. Velazquez. THE SPINNERS. *Madrid*   89

35. Velazquez. THE MAIDS OF HONOR. *Madrid*   92

36. Goya. THE MAJA NUDE. *Madrid*   96

37. Goya. THE SHOOTING. *Madrid*   98

38. Ancient Roman. THESEUS AFTER KILLING
      THE MINOTAUR. *Naples*   106

39. Ancient Roman. HERCULES' SON SUCKLED BY
      THE HIND. *Naples*   109

40. Ancient Roman. LANDSCAPE WITH FIGURES.
      Naples   111

41. Ancient Roman. PASIPHAE AND THE BULL.
      Rome   115

42. Ancient Roman. THE ATTACK OF THE LES-
      TRIGONI. *Rome*   119

43. Michelangelo. THE CREATION OF MAN. *Rome*   122

44. Michelangelo. THE FALL OF MAN. *Rome*   124

45. Raphael. THE SCHOOL OF ATHENS. *Rome*   127

46. Piero della Francesca. THE QUEEN OF SHEBA
      ADORING THE CROSS. *Arezzo*   132

47. Duccio. THE THREE MARYS AT THE TOMB.
      Siena   135

48. Botticelli. THE BIRTH OF VENUS. *Florence*   138

49. Giovanni Bellini. ALLEGORY OF PURGATORY.
      Florence   141

FIGURE   PAGE

50. Pollaiuolo. HERCULES KILLING THE HYDRA.
    Florence   144

51. Raphael. MADONNA OF THE CHAIR. *Florence*   148

52. Filippo Lippi. MADONNA AND CHILD. *Florence*   150

53. Byzantine School. CRUCIFIXION. *Florence*   153

54. Byzantine School. ST. JOHN THE BAPTIST.
    Florence   155

55. Masaccio. THE TRIBUTE MONEY. *Florence*   157

56. Fra Angelico. THE ANNUNCIATION. *Florence*   160

57. Benozzo Gozzoli. THE JOURNEY OF THE
    MAGI. *Florence*   162

58. Giotto. THE DESCENT FROM THE CROSS.
    Padua.   164

59. Giotto. THE RESURRECTION OF LAZARUS.
    Padua   167

60. Titian. THE DEPOSITION. *Venice*   171

61. Carpaccio. THE LEGEND OF ST. URSULA.
    Venice   173

62. Basaiti. THE CALLING OF THE SONS OF ZEBE-
    DEE. *Venice*   176

63. Tintoretto. THE LAST SUPPER. *Venice*   179

64. Tintoretto. THE ASCENSION. *Venice*   182

65. Veronese. THE RAPE OF EUROPA. *Venice*   185

66. Byzantine School. STORIES OF JESUS. *Venice*   187

List of Illustrations

FIGURE   PAGE

67. Brueghel. THE RETURN OF THE HUNTERS.
    Vienna   193

68. Jordaens. THE BEAN-KING'S FEAST. *Vienna*   196

69. Holbein. JANE SEYMOUR. *Vienna*   198

70. Rubens. LANDSCAPE WITH PHILEMON AND
    BAUCIS. *Vienna*   200

71. Vermeer. THE ARTIST IN HIS STUDIO. *Vienna*   204

72. Dürer. KNIGHT, DEATH AND DEVIL. *Vienna*   207

73. Dürer. THE PRODIGAL SON. *Vienna*   209

74. Rembrandt. EULENSPIEGEL. *Vienna*   210

75. Grünewald. CHRIST MOCKED. *Munich*   214

76. Brueghel. FOOL'S PARADISE. *Munich*   216

77. Rubens. THE RAPE OF THE DAUGHTERS OF
    LEUCIPPUS. *Munich*   218

78. Rubens. HÉLÈNE FOURMENT WITH HER
    CHILD. *Munich*   222

79. Manet. THE BOAT. *Munich*   225

80. Cézanne. STILL LIFE. *Munich*   227

81. Van Gogh. VIEW OF ARLES. *Munich*   230

82. Giorgione. THE SLEEPING VENUS. *Dresden*   233

83. Courbet. THE STONE-BREAKERS. *Dresden*   236

84. Petrus Cristus. PORTRAIT OF A YOUNG GIRL.
    Berlin   239

85. Cranach. APOLLO AND DIANA. *Berlin*   241

FIGURE   PAGE

86. Patinir. REST ON THE FLIGHT TO EGYPT.
    Berlin   243

87. Hals. HILLE BOBBE, THE WITCH OF HAAR-
    LEM. *Berlin*   245

88. Rembrandt. THE MAN WITH THE GOLD HEL-
    MET. *Berlin*   247

89. Titian. VENUS WITH THE ORGAN-PLAYER.
    Berlin   250

90. Correggio. LEDA AND THE SWAN. *Berlin*   253

91. Domenico Veneziano. PORTRAIT OF A GIRL.
    Berlin   255

92. Roger van der Weyden. THE SEVEN SACRA-
    MENTS. *Antwerp*   258

93. Dieric Bouts. THE JUSTICE OF OTTO. *Brussels*   261

94. Memling. THE MARTYRDOM OF ST. SEBAS-
    TIAN. *Brussels*   263

95. Bosch. THE TEMPTATION OF ST. ANTHONY.
    Brussels   265

96. Rembrandt. THE NIGHT WATCH. *Amsterdam*   268

97. de Hooch. THE PANTRY. *Amsterdam*   271

98. Salomon van Ruisdael. THE BRIDGE. *The
    Hague*   274

99. Veronese. THE FINDING OF MOSES. *Leningrad*   278

100. Gauguin. WOMAN WITH A PIECE OF FRUIT.
     Moscow   283

INTRODUCTION

1. Different Values in Painting

ALMOST anyone can get some enjoyment from pictures, without reading books about them. In a great museum like the Louvre, no one can fail to find something that will interest and please at first sight, with no special effort. A visitor who has paid little or no attention to art before will probably find most of the pictures there uninteresting, and will wonder, if he hears about it, why the critics have praised some of them so enthusiastically. But he will stop to admire others in which the subject means something to him, and in which the scenes or figures are accurately and clearly represented. One will bring to mind some event or character in history or legend; another some place where he has travelled or would like to travel; another shows a beautiful, or an odd and impressive face. This is entertainment enough to fill an idle hour or two.

To be strictly just in giving credit for this pleasant hour, however, he should award it not so much to the pictures as to his own past reading and experience about the subjects they represent, or to his own power to dream interesting fancies. Very little in the way of a picture is enough to arouse particular memories; the mere label, " Napoleon at Elba," " Romeo and Juliet," or " Child Praying " is enough to start an active imagination off in paths of memory or sentiment. The barest representation of the subject will help still more, and one is apt to credit the picture, unconsciously, for the whole brief experience.

If a person who has enjoyed looking at pictures for their subject-matter ever reads a book of modern art criticism, he is apt to be surprised and unconvinced. He is likely to be told in such a book that he has been looking at pictures in the wrong way; that the right way is to ignore subject-matter, and pay attention only to *form* — a vague and forbidding word. It seems that the critic is trying to take away a very real source of pleasure, and to substitute some difficult brand of mental discipline.

As it happens, the present book goes to no such extreme. In almost all the comments on pictures in the following pages, some reference is made to their particular " expressive " or " representative " values; to the sort of associations they tend to arouse in the observer. In regard to a portrait by Leonardo da Vinci or by Rembrandt, for example, mention is made of its interest as representing an unusual type of character; in regard to a fanciful scene by Watteau or Fragonard, of the particular mood of gay luxury it expresses, which is typical of the age that produced it. Much argument is still going on in critical circles about the relative stress which should be laid on expressive values, as contrasted with those of pure design. There is no need to go into it here. The viewpoint of this book, it can be stated briefly, is that subject-matter need not and should not be ignored entirely; that the observer is right in allowing his imagination to respond to at least the main, direct suggestions which the artist is trying to convey: those which are not mere accidental, personal associations of his own, but somehow bound definitely to the form of the picture itself, through widely established bonds of human nature and social experience. There is no need to deny oneself, in the long run, any kind of pleasure which pictures afford, and none is necessarily inconsistent with any other.

After this has been said, the other side remains to be emphasized. No one needs to read a book on art appreciation to learn how to enjoy the subject-matter of pictures. That sort of pleasure comes easily enough, through one's general experience and education. The pleasures of appreciating form do not come so readily to most people, in our age at least. Abstract and difficult as the word sounds, it stands for a very real kind of interest and enjoyment, not in the least abstract or tedious; a vast world of experience highly valuable for its own sake, which many people miss as completely as a deaf person misses music. Some can never enjoy it, lacking proper eyesight or other necessary qualifications, physical or temperamental. But to persons who have the necessary capacities (and one never knows before trying) the critic is justified in offering the friendly advice to make the same first effort which he has found decidedly worth while. And he is right in adding that a necessary step in that direction is to learn how to ignore subject-matter entirely at times. For a while, at least, the beginner must consciously restrain his imagination from wandering off on associated bypaths, for the reason that such daydreams are sure to distract his attention from the picture in front of his eyes.

Almost everyone appreciates form in pictures to some extent, without conscious effort. Children like bright colors, and grown people like softly blended ones, without being told to do so. There is no great difficulty in distinguishing between a picture that is evenly balanced in composition and one in which everything is over at the side. Such ideas and likings are a start toward appreciation; they are harmful only when negatively applied — when used to condemn and reject any picture that does not conform to a few narrow standards. A person who says, " I don't want to learn to like that," injures nobody but himself.

What a book on art appreciation can and should do, for a person of limited training in art, is to show him some additional ways in which pictures can probably interest and please him, if he will let them. What are these additional ways?

For one thing, it may be able to call his attention to some finer points he has missed in familiar pictures, through not having stopped to look closely enough. There are subtle and delicate qualities in the shading and color of some artists, that do not strike the eye at once. Effort and training are necessary to develop an eye that is sensitive to fine distinctions.

Again, many pictures are extremely complex in plan of organization, and a hasty glance, with attention wandering elsewhere, is not enough to show the inter-relation of parts. As a symphony is built together of melodies, chord-progressions, modulations in key and other factors, so a picture can be built of certain repeated lines, colors, solid objects, light and dark areas, each put down with care as a part of some unified design. To follow these many parts in detail, to see how a certain theme — some distinctive, curving line, some particular color — is repeated here and there, varied a little to avoid monotony, contrasted suddenly with a radically different theme, bound up with it in some consistent way, and the whole picture thus made into a new, consistent world of its own — this is one of the greatest enjoyments that the world of art can afford. There is no way of proving to the uninitiated that it is worth doing at all. In general terms, it sounds unattractive; and even to read a particular picture-analysis, and look here for this line, there for that spot of color, is not very exciting in itself. Words are the only way, however, in which an author not present to point with his hand can call the reader's attention to specific details. For the ultimate justification, he can only point to the testimony of countless artists and lovers of art in every age, who have found such playing with visual forms to be one of the most exciting and fascinating activities that life affords.

One more thing which books on appreciation can do, but do not always attempt, is to acquaint the reader with a variety of unfamiliar forms of art — those of remote civilizations, and of eccentric individual geniuses in his own. People in China accept their traditional forms as a matter of course. We are accustomed to the Greek, Florentine and Dutch traditions most of all, and anything else is apt to seem at first crude, ugly or distorted. In time, a person of flexible mind can accustom himself to strange, exotic conventions, and feel at ease with them. Many have done so in recent years with Japanese prints, and no longer feel them as crude or distorted. Each time we come to grasp what an unfamiliar artist or school is trying to say in pictures, we have learned a new language and enlarged our experience. We also find, as a rule, that all the visible world outside of art has become a little more interesting. We now notice in nature, in the fields and in crowds of people, forms like those which the artist has called to our attention. There is endless interest in observing, selecting and rearranging them into imaginary pictures of our own.

With these aims in mind, stress is laid throughout this book on the limitless variety of pictorial forms, and on the value of learning to enjoy each for what it is, not condemning it because it is not something else. There is no need of hurry in arriving at complete, final verdicts about a picture's value — whether it is " really " beautiful or ugly, better or worse than some other.

That does not imply a complete lack of standards, a too tolerant belief that any picture is as good as any other. After learning to appreciate many forms and traditions, the student gradually comes to see that certain artists are trying to do about the same thing, and that one has succeeded more completely than another. One artist is comparatively original; another is merely imitating him, with something left out.

One organizes his materials more harmoniously; the other has left certain conflicting and confusing factors, which defeat the main purpose he is trying to achieve. One interests and satisfies us in many ways at once; another in only a few; one in rather trivial ways, soon tiresome; another in ways that appeal to something more fundamental and permanent in us as individuals, and in all human nature.

Thus general standards can be worked out experimentally, as we go along. But aesthetic values are so varied and controversial that it is well to go slowly in formulating definite standards and applying them rigorously. There are no absolute rules or authorities now to distinguish good art from bad, and perhaps never will be. In the mean time, a much more practical and directly rewarding task is to look around open-mindedly, to perceive and enjoy the rich profusion of different values in art which our cultural heritage places before us.*

2. A Questionnaire for Picture-analysis

This outline is intended for the use of readers who may wish to analyze pictures for themselves, from the standpoint of form, with more than ordinary care and thoroughness. It consists of a series of questions, to be read through and answered in the presence of any given picture. Its aim is to aid in detailed, systematic observation, through directing the reader's attention to the many different elements which go to make up a complex design. In addition, it aims to help the reader make up his own mind about a picture's merits, through taking up one by one several specific points on which it can be judged. For a beginner it may be well to answer all or most of the questions in the order given, with about the

* The general question of standards of value in art is more thoroughly discussed in *Scientific Method in Aesthetics*, by the author (1928.)

same degree of care. Later on, he will discover that for different pictures, different questions are most important. He will learn to " size up " a new picture more quickly in a general way, and will alter his plan of analysis to suit. If he sees that color is most important in the work at hand, he will concentrate his attention on the use of color; if line, he will stress that. The analyses given in this book follow no set order, and mention only the qualities that seem most important in each case; to do otherwise would be useless and tedious. But at first the untrained observer is apt to look only for the few qualities in painting with which he is familiar. His main effort should be to keep looking at the same picture from different points of view, to find if possible some important qualities he has been overlooking.

A. FIRST IMPRESSIONS OF THE PICTURE AS A WHOLE

1. What is most striking, interesting or unusual about the picture at first sight? What is most pleasing? Least pleasing? Why?

2. What seems to have been the artist's chief aim or interest in this picture? (E.g., line or color pattern, dramatic narrative, facial expression, religious or other associations.)

3. Is the picture at first sight more interesting for its design or for the subject represented? What, in general, is most noteworthy about each? Does the picture seem to combine and harmonize both of these kinds of appeal?

4. Of what main parts or elements is the design composed? In what general way are they put together? (E.g., three solid figures arranged in a pyramidal group against a flat contrasting background.)

5. What lines, colors, shadows, masses or other elements in design are most conspicuous? Are some of them (e.g., a certain angle, or a certain shade of red) repeated several

times, with only slight variation? Are two or more very
different colors, shapes of line or other elements contrasted
with each other?

B. LINE

1. Are the outlines of things conspicuous? Do they stand
out as separate, detached strokes of the brush, distinct from
areas on both sides of them? Do they appear only as edges
or contours of surfaces or objects? Are such contours sharp
and clear-cut, or blurred by soft shadows or gradual color
blends? Are there wholly isolated lines, which do not serve
to mark the limits of any area of light or color?

2. Are the lines rhythmic, full of repeated shapes? Is their
general appearance smooth, flowing, graceful, delicate, flexible, undulating, swirling? Is it rough and jagged, stiff, angular, heavy or static? Is it weak, aimless, confused? Different
in different places?

3. What particular linear theme, if any, such as a characteristic curve, seems to dominate in the design? Does it
dominate through frequent repetition, or through large size,
or other emphasis? Where is it repeated? Is it slightly varied
in size, shape or direction, or through being embodied in
differently lighted or colored objects?

4. What other very different linear theme is there? (E.g.,
a series of sharp angles as contrasted with a series of flowing
curves.) How is this one repeated and varied? Are some
lines intermediate in shape between the two, serving as
gradual transitions between them? Are there more than two
definite themes?

5. Are these themes combined in a single, unified pattern?
How? (E.g., through being arranged in symmetrical opposition, intertwined in a continuous arabesque, fitted together into a pyramid or circle, or caught up in some general
swirling or zig-zag movement.) Does this pattern extend

through the whole picture, or is it limited to certain parts? Is it independent of the spots of color, solid objects and other factors, or do these also join in the same arrangement?

6. Are the linear contours of things reproduced from nature with great accuracy? (E.g., bodily proportions, perspective.) In minute, elaborate detail, or with some simplifications and emphasis? With great alteration or distortion?

7. Is the result to bring out some rhythm or pattern? To bring out some distinctive feature of the object represented, as in a caricature, or a portrait that accents some peculiarity of physique or personality? To represent some action or situation more tersely? To express some definite emotion or mood of the artist?

C. LIGHT AND DARK

1. Are there distinct light areas and dark areas? Where? Are the light parts concentrated or scattered? The dark?

2. Is there strong contrast between one and the other, from extreme to extreme? Are there only a few definite shades, or many intermediate degrees of lightness and darkness? Are transitions between them sudden, sharp-edged, or soft and gradual?

3. Do the lightest spots when looked at together, or the darkest spots when looked at together, combine to form a pattern? (E.g., do they stand out as indicating parts of a triangle, circle, spiral or some other definite shape?) Do all the different shades combine into one complex pattern?

4. Is there an effect of real illumination, as from the sun or a lamp? Are the light spots of the picture made chiefly by reflected highlights or direct gleams from a source of light? Are the dark spots formed by cast shadows? Partly or entirely in other ways, as by white and black garments, or tree-trunks against snow?

5. Are the shadows soft, velvety, delicate, full of subtle gradations, faint reflections, vaguely suggested shapes and textures? Dense, black, murky, flat and shiny? Are the high-lights also subtly graded in intensity, or bare and uniform?

6. Is there an effect of outdoor sunlight, moonlight, lamp-light? From one concentrated source? If from more than one, how are the reflections and shadows from them distinguished or blended? Is the light direct, intense, diffused, clear, broken, filtered through leaves, flickering, cloudy, dulled, glaring?

7. Is an effect produced of soft, pervasive atmosphere, luminous glow, or rich surface texture? By subtle light gradations alone, without the aid of color? Are light transitions closely bound up with those of color, or independent?

8. Is some kind of illumination represented with great accuracy, as it would appear in a real scene? Are lights or shadows intensified, made unnaturally bright or dark? Are shadows omitted, or placed where they could not possibly fall? Made sketchy, rough, fragmentary? Are long streaks of light and shadow used as lines to define contours or directions of movement?

9. Is the result realistic? Is it to bring out some pattern or the shape of some important object? Does the quality of light produce some distinctive emotional tone, such as gloominess, cheerfulness, weirdness, mystery, agitation?

D. COLOR

1. What is the immediate general effect of the picture's coloring at a distance, without regard to details of pattern or representation? Is it dull, dark, sombre, bleak or bare? Is it vivid, intense, clear, pure, jewel-like? Warm or cool? Crude, violent, barbaric, clashing, glaring? Dingy, muddy, acid, tawdry? Quiet, subdued, soft, delicate? Rich, gorgeous,

rainbow-like? Monotonous, confused, tiresome? Do different parts of the picture vary notably in these respects?

2. When a particular small area of color is looked at closely, does it seem monotonously uniform within its own limits? Is it rich, iridescent, shot through with glints of light, subtly varied in tint? Is it built up of various films of paint, the lower showing in places through the upper? Of contrasting small brush-strokes side by side? Of colors partly but not wholly blended? Do different areas vary in these respects? Does it make much difference how far away one stands?

3. What hue or tint is dominant, most important? Because of its brightness? Its wide distribution? Its central or focal position? What color is next in importance? What minor notes of color are there? Are there many different hues?

4. Is each different color enclosed within definite linear boundaries? Strongly contrasted with its neighbors? Do some colors, or all, blend into each other gradually, as if melting and overflowing linear boundaries? Do they blend completely, into one almost uniform surface, or is there a moderate amount of contrast?

5. In regard to each principal hue employed: where is it repeated in separate spots? What variation is there between the spots of a certain color? Where is it made lighter? Darker? More intense? Duller? Where is it mixed a little with another tint? With still a different tint? (E.g., a green which varies here toward blue, there toward yellow, somewhere else toward violet.) Are some areas neutral, intermediate between two principal contrasting hues? Are some intermediate in shade, and in intensity, between the principal color-areas? If not, is the result monotonous? Confused? Clashing?

6. Do the scattered spots of a certain color combine to form

a pattern when looked at together? Is this pattern otherwise indicated, as by linear outlines, or does it depend on color alone, so that it would disappear in a photograph? What sort of pattern is it, as to complexity, and method of inter-relating parts?

7. Do color repetitions link together parts of the picture that would be otherwise unrelated? Do color contrasts help distinguish parts that would otherwise be vague or confused? Are some parts of the picture unincluded in the main color-pattern?

8. Does the juxtaposition of certain colors seem to affect the quality of each? E.g., when a hand is placed over one area, do its neighbors seem different? Less luminous? More or less agreeable? Do areas which are weak or unpleasant in color, when examined individually, become satisfying when seen as parts of a group? Could individual areas be much altered in color without weakening the effect of unity?

9. Do the colors rise to a climax of richness, intensity or brightness at some point or points? Are there minor as well as major accents and climaxes? Do other colors contrast with them and lead up to them in continuous, orderly progressions?

10. Are there fairly distinct subordinate groups or color-chords, combinations which occur together repeatedly in small areas? How are they related to each other through the picture? How varied? Is the picture built up of distinct sections or panels, each a distinct pattern or texture in itself? (E.g., are some sections of a uniform flat color, others striped, shadowed, flowered, mottled?) Are there repetitions of similar sections?

11. Does color seem to be a superficial, unnecessary addition, laid on after the picture has been basically constructed of lines, lights and darks? How much would the picture lose in black and white?

12. Is color realistic, made to seem an inseparable part of

objects, permeating their inner substance, through subtle variations of light and tint? Are the distinctive qualities of different substances brought out clearly? (E.g., a hand as contrasted with stone or wood.) Are certain textures (e.g., metallic, silky, woolly) repeated, varied and contrasted as themes?

13. Are the colors blended into a soft, deep, translucent atmosphere? Is it warm, Venetian, glowing, red-and-gold? Cool, blue, pale, clear, crystalline, fresh, silvery? Dense, hazy, misty, dim? Shimmering, sparkling, glittering? Does the atmosphere serve to unify all parts of the picture? Are certain parts unincluded within it?

14. Are shadows dead, shallow, muddy grays or browns? Richly tinted, but the same in general hue as the highlights? Contrasting in hue? (E.g., rose highlights with olive shadows.) With what effect on realism? General richness of texture? Definite pattern?

15. Is emphasis placed on the surface reflections of sunlight on colored objects? Is broken-color technique used? Is the local, intrinsic color of any object altered by reflection from other colored surfaces? (E.g., a yellow dress by grass near it.) Is the result realistic? More than naturally brilliant?

16. Does the coloring help express some distinctive mood or emotion? (E.g., gay, martial, funereal, weird, austere, majestic, agitated.) Is this consistent with the rest of the picture? With the usual associations of the subject?

E. MASS

1. Do objects appear to stand out from their backgrounds as solid, three-dimensional masses? In clear-cut, high relief? In low relief? Are they delicate, fragile, lacy? Soft, vaporous, vague, shapeless? Are some or all objects flat? (E.g., silhouettes against a fire.)

2. Do various objects differ much in degree of solidity? Does this help emphasize important objects, or balance weights?

3. Are the various parts of an individual object (e.g., separate garments and limbs) clearly distinct, or do they blend gradually? Do they produce an effect of design through repeating a certain kind of plane, such as triangular folds in a garment?

4. Is the illusion of solidity produced by light and shadow alone? By perspective? By the advancing or receding quality of certain colors?

5. Are the shapes and contours of objects accurately represented? In detail, or with selective emphasis to bring out essentials, such as the basic structure of the body?

6. Are shapes distorted to bring out some pattern? (E.g., by elongating limbs, or exaggerating muscles, to produce a repetition of similar shapes.) Are they flattened, to bring out surface pattern of lines and colors?

7. Are shapes distorted to accent some peculiarity in the thing represented, such as strength, fatness, agility? To express some emotion such as pain, ecstasy or frenzied effort?

F. SPACE

1. Do all parts of the picture appear to be at the same distance from the eye, or is there an illusion of deep space and different distances? Is there a shallow inward view, stopped at a short distance, as by a curtain or wall? A definite, large area, like a public square, or a vista that recedes into infinite distance?

2. How is the illusion of depth, if any, produced? By converging perspective lines, lights and shadows, variations in size, different degrees of distinctness, color-contrasts?

3. Are the relative distances of objects clear or vague? Clearer nearby? Unnaturally clear, even in the distance?

4. Is the surface of the picture divided into similar parts, such as triangles, rectangles, ellipses?

5. Does some one figure or other object dominate the picture, through size, conspicuous light or color, or position at focus of converging lines? At or near the center? Is symmetry preserved, exactly or approximately? Is the main part far to one side? If so, is balance restored by some compensating factor on the other, such as a bright light or color, or several small objects? Is balance definitely destroyed? Does this seem unintentional, or consistent with the spirit of the whole, as in a deliberate effect of unrest or casualness?

6. Is there a distinct division into foreground, middle-ground and background? With more than natural contrast in light or color?

7. Is the arrangement of objects in space haphazard? Could they be shifted without weakening the unity of the whole? Are they vague, confused, in relative position?

8. Is there a definite, step-by-step recession away from the eye? At fairly regular intervals, with rhythmic effect? In groups, or individually?

9. Are some regions in deep space over-crowded? Are some empty, bare, uninteresting? Are objects distributed through the area taken in, to fill it and mark it off clearly?

10. Are the planes of different objects arranged in space at different angles, to make a design? (E.g., roof-tops, hills, dishes on a table.) With definite repetition, variation, contrast?

11. Are natural laws, such as perspective and gravitation, ignored in any way? (E.g., by raising horizon line or corner of table; showing together various moments or aspects of a scene, which could not be seen together in nature.) For a decorative purpose, as to give a tapestry-like flat background? For expressive or narrative reasons?

12. Are some figures represented as moving in space?

With convincing illusion of movement, or stiffly and wood-
enly? According to natural laws, or in impossible, fantastic
ways?

13. Are the suggested movements of various figures related together in some way? Only as representing elements
in the same story? By some continuous rhythm of lines or
masses? Do light and color contrasts help the sense of movement? Are the movements mainly in unison, in opposition,
in confusion? Do they lead up to some emphatic, significant
gesture or attitude as a climax? (E.g., the dead body in a
Pietà; the ascent in an *Assumption.*) Do they produce an
effect of dynamic design, as in an organized group dance?
With excessive regularity, or with variation and contrast?

G. UNITY OF DESIGN

1. Which of the above factors, and which quality in its use,
seems to contribute most to the intended effect of design?
Which seems to be most original, and in what way? Which
are notably weak? Imitative?

2. Does some one factor stand out in isolation from the
whole? With an effect of conflict or confusion? Of intended
emphasis or specialized, limited mode of appeal? Are the
other factors unrelated, inconsistent, or merely subordinated?

3. Do line, light, color, mass and space all coöperate
actively and harmoniously? Do all the particular qualities,
rhythms and subordinate patterns noted above contribute
definitely to one cumulative effect?

3. An Outline of the History of Painting

I. *Prehistoric.* Old Stone Age, about 15,000 B.C. Southern France and northern Spain. Engravings on bone imple-
ments, and colored chalk drawings of animals and dancers,

on cave walls. Simplified, rhythmic, terse in expressing bodily structure and movement.

II. *Egyptian*. Works of the Fourth Dynasty (2900–2750 B.C.) found at Meidum; of the Eighteenth Dynasty (1580–1350 B.C.) at Thebes. Painting on tomb walls, of birds and animals, industries, battles, processions. Flat, bright, contrasting colors; monotonous repetition of stiff, simple angles and curves; occasional naturalistic drawing of animals in movement, mostly in profile.

III. *Greek and Roman. Minoan* phase *c.* 1500 B.C. in Crete; frescoes of sports, animals, processions; similar in form to Egyptian, often with more irregularity and animation. *Greek* phase 8th to 2nd century B.C., with center at Athens. Vase painting, developed from crude geometrical ornament to lifelike human and animal figures, graceful, rhythmic, decorative, with light-dark contrast; little shadowing or depth. Other painting, on flat surfaces, advanced in 5th and 4th centuries B.C. toward naturalism of shading, anatomy, perspective. Leaders: Polygnotus, Zeuxis, Apelles. *Roman* phase 2nd century B.C. to 3rd century A.D. Development of Greek naturalism, with deeper space and atmospheric coloring.

IV. *Early Christian, Byzantine, Gothic*. First phase under Roman Empire, with religious frescoes and mosaics, some animated, solidly modelled with shadows, others tending to flat stylization. Second phase under Byzantine Empire (4th to 15th centuries) with centers at Constantinople, Kieff, Athens, Sicily, Ravenna, Venice; mosaics and book miniatures, mostly religious; tendency to flat, rigid shapes, decorated in bright, contrasting colors, blending Roman and Eastern influences; book illuminations more animated, sketchy, individual. Third (Gothic) phase, in middle ages, with centers in England, Ireland, France, Italy, Germany. Manuscript illuminations continued, with tendency in fourteenth century toward lighter, simpler painting; increasing realism; foliage ornament. Byzantine tradition continued in Russia till modern times.

V. *Oriental. China.* Painting flourished in T'ang, Sung and Ming Dynasties (4th to 14th centuries A.D.) Buddhist frescoes; painting on silk scrolls of landscapes, animals, portraits, in finely expressive, freely varied rhythmic lines and graded lights and darks; little or no modelling with cast shadows or exact perspective, but both solidity and depth suggested by other means; color rather superficial, often omitted. Typical leaders: Ku K'ai-chih, Li Lung Mien, Ma Yuan. *Japan.* Flourished 15th to 18th centuries, at first under Chinese influence; Buddhist figures, landscapes, action drawings, decorative costume portraits, ornamented folded screens. Typical leaders: Sesshu, Korin. Prints developed as a popular art in 18th century; leaders Hokusai, Hiroshige, Utamaro. *Persia.* Miniatures and calligraphy in books developed 15th to 18th centuries; bright, contrasting colors, with flattening and distortion of perspective; some finely rhythmic line drawings, under Indian and Chinese influence. *India.* Early Buddhist frescoes at Ajanta, 3rd century B.C. to 7th A.D., with illustrations of stories in simple, monumental drawing. Rajput and Mughal schools, 16th to 18th centuries, combining Persian and native styles.

VI. *Early Renaissance.* 14th and 15th centuries, especially in *Florence* and *central Italy, Flanders, Germany* and *France.* Revival of Greek and Roman tradition in painting: realistic drawing, tinting and modelling of human body, with cast shadows; designs formed by arranging bodies at different distances in deep space. Strong influence of classical sculpture, producing idealized human figures, at first solemnly religious, later more secular and naturalistic. Coloring usually superficial; sometimes brightly decorative, through survival of Byzantine feeling; sometimes dull and monotonous, through specialized emphasis on drawing, perspective, light and shade. In Flanders, special attention to small, realistic miniature detail; early use of oils. In Italy, dry fresco and tempera surfaces at first, oils later. Italian and local influences blended in France and Germany to produce distinctive styles in portraiture and religious subjects. Leaders: in *Italy*, Giotto, Duccio, Masaccio, Piero della Francesca, Uccello, Fra Angelico, Filippo Lippi, Botticelli, Leonardo da Vinci, Michelangelo, Raphael; in *Flanders* and the *Netherlands*, Hubert and Jan Van Eyck, Roger Van der Weyden, Bouts, Memling; in *France*, Jean Fouquet; in *Germany*, Lochner.

VII. *Late Renaissance*. Leadership assumed by *Venice* and *northern Italy*, through development of oil medium into richly colored, softly blended, realistic textures and glowing atmospheres. Founders of the school, contemporary with later Florentines, lived in late 15th and early 16th centuries: Mantegna, Giovanni Bellini, Carpaccio, Giorgione. Later Venetians, 2nd half of 16th century: Titian, Tintoretto, Paolo Veronese. *Germans* active in the early 16th century: Dürer, Grünewald, Cranach, Holbein; closer to Florentine and Gothic styles than to Venetian. In *Flanders:* Bosch, Brueghel.

VIII. *Seventeenth century*. Italian dominance ended, and vigorous national schools arise in *Spain*, El Greco, Velazquez; *France*, Le Nain, Poussin, Claude Lorrain; *Flanders* and *Holland*, Rubens, Hals, Rembrandt, Vermeer, Van Goyen, the Ruysdaels. Landscape interest strong in France and Holland. Venetian coloring developed along many different lines, combined with local traditions; e.g., with tendency to cooler, clearer tones of green and blue in Holland and France. Specialization along individual lines, with frequent tendency to simplify, abbreviate strokes, or limit range of colors. In Spain and in northern Europe, influence of classical revival wanes; humble peasant and middle-class figures, plain rural farmlands and home interiors, gradually replace Greek and Christian deities, noble personages and magnificent parks, as subjects. Forms also less prevailingly classical, often avoiding delicate grace and neat pattern, to stress blunt, irregular, plainly substantial shapes and textures. Dignity and grandeur are conveyed in simple terms.

IX. *Eighteenth century.* Loss of simplicity and strength; tendency to lightness and delicacy, to elaborate surface decoration, to expressions of gayety, luxury, sentimentality. *French* court painting most influential: Watteau, Boucher, Fragonard; Chardin continues Dutch simplicity and substantial strength. In *Spain,* Goya stands out as original and versatile. In *England,* much sentimental, prettified portraiture of aristocracy and smiling children; Constable, Blake, Turner, at beginning of 19th century, carry on more vigorous traditions.

X. *Nineteenth century.* *France* preëminent throughout. Classical school of David and Ingres stresses severe linear drawing and Florentine sculptural modelling, with drab color. Delacroix, romanticist, follows Rubens and Venetian tradition, in rich melting color and swirling energy. Barbizon school, of 1830's, prevailingly Dutch in inspiration, painting rustic landscapes, peasants, cattle; Corot, however, follows Claude Lorrain and the Venetians. Courbet, in the fifties, champions naturalism against both classicism and romanticism; revives the Spanish style of broad, rough, simplified strokes, with massive contours. Manet follows, but in later years joins the impressionists, Monet, Sisley, Pissarro, in stressing sunlight reflections and iridescent atmospheres, produced by broken color technique. Cézanne, Renoir and Seurat, after practicing impressionism, organize its brilliant colors into solid objects in clear, deep space, thus combining it with Renaissance values. At end of century, other early post-impressionists — Van Gogh, Gauguin, Degas, Henri Rousseau — strike out on various paths, reviving different primitive or exotic styles, emphasizing free distortion of natural model to produce distinctive design, or to stress distinctive characteristics.

XI. *Twentieth century*. Paris continues as center, and French as dominant group, with Matisse combining Persian, impressionist and other elements, and Derain reviving different primitive styles. Foreigners residing in Paris are influential in post-impressionist group: e.g., Picasso (Spanish), Chirico (Italian); others German, Russian, Polish, Dutch, Japanese. No one dominant tendency or type; much adaptation of primitive and exotic traditions; individual experiment on highly specialized problems of form. Search for bizarre distortions, unusual and striking designs; deliberate avoidance of appeal through realism or associations of subject-matter. Vigorous groups in Germany, Russia, England, America, much influenced by Cézanne and Van Gogh. Cosmopolitanism and individualism; blending of all past traditions, and of distinctive national traits.

CHAPTER I

ENGLAND

THERE is no better place than London to begin a survey of
Europe's picture galleries. For anyone who is not versed in
the languages and customs of the Continent, there is an
obvious advantage in being able to find what one is looking for, and read the title of it when it is found, without
calling in the services of a guide or a dictionary. More important, even to the seasoned traveller, is the fact that
London contains a few good examples of practically every
great school, age and type of painting. With little travel
or inconvenience, one can readily get a bird's-eye view
of the whole field of art, and a look at some fairly typical
works by a large proportion of the great artists of history.
A few days wisely distributed there will give a broad if
not thorough acquaintance with the chief traditions in painting, past and present, European and oriental. This will make
it possible to decide with more confidence which particular
ones to study more thoroughly later. Then a glance through
the other chapters of this book will be of assistance in learning where any individual artist is to be found at his best.
For that reason, an unusually wide variety of examples has
been selected for illustration and discussion in this first
chapter.

The principal museum in London is the famous *National Gallery*, at Trafalgar Square. It contains the European old masters, including those British works which have come to be regarded as classics. The *Millbank* branch of the National Gallery, formerly called the Tate Collection, is devoted to more recent works of less established reputation, especially British and French. The *Wallace Collection*, at Manchester Square, is composed largely of eighteenth century French, with a few excellent examples of the Dutch and other schools. The *British Museum*, in Bloomsbury, is often neglected by travellers interested in pictures. It is given special emphasis here because of its primitive, medieval and oriental paintings, which are not only fascinating in themselves, but strongly influential in the art of today. A few smaller galleries are given briefer mention.

The National Gallery at Trafalgar Square

The collection is arranged in rooms according to national schools: Italian in the center, Spanish, Flemish and Dutch on the right as one enters, French, German and British on the left. We begin with careful examination of a few outstanding, and very different, types of picture.

PAOLO UCCELLO. THE ROUT OF SAN ROMANO. (*Fig. 2; No. 583* *.)

To the decorative charm of medieval tapestry, this picture adds the depth and solidity of early Renaissance painting. Though this touch of realism strengthens the total form, the picture's distinctive appeal is still decorative, through its brilliant design of contrasting themes in line,

* These numbers, following the figure number, refer to the number of the picture in each museum.

FIG. 2. THE ROUT OF SAN ROMANO
By Uccello

light and color. In line, the themes are long straight lances, round oranges and harness-plates, and the wavy curves of prancing horses. All these shapes are echoed with variation in the long lines of the hills and pennants, and in the shorter ones of the men in armor. Following the traditions of heraldic design, there are constant sudden contrasts between various distinct shades, with no soft melting transitions; also between the sheen of metals and the tints of other substances, and between plain and richly brocaded textures. The color is laid on in broad, superficial, contrasting areas, some dull and neutral, to bring out such accented spots as the leader's gorgeous head-dress. Among details worth noticing are the exquisitely chiselled, cameo-like profile of the boy behind the leader; the block-like, sculptural carving of the horses, and the obvious but not quite successful attempt at realistic perspective in the fallen soldiers and broken lances. The picture's expressive value is its stirring air of knightly panoply. But its effort to portray the clash of arms is weakened by the stiffness of the gestures. Bodily movement is not well represented, but there is a more abstract, decorative sort of movement, lively and crackling, in the interplay of themes in the design.

TITIAN. BACCHUS AND ARIADNE. (*Fig. 3; No. 35.*)

Here the sense of bodily movement is conveyed with a fluency which had come from several generations of technical study after Uccello. Its achievement demands not only skill in copying the appearance of the body, but the more artistic power to select and emphasize exactly those positions, contours and shadowings of limbs and muscle that will suggest most vividly the type of action intended. An actual photograph of action will rarely do this. Here the type to be expressed is the Bacchanalian procession, traditionally one.

FIG. 3. BACCHUS AND ARIADNE
By Titian

of divinely intoxicated revelry. It has one pervasive rhythm of clashing cymbals and swaying limbs, but it is not a dance in unison — something between that and a disorderly rout. Every figure has a different attitude, but all are swept onward in a continuous flow of waving arms and leaping, marching legs, to a climax in the weightless flying god, and an ending in the shrinking figure of Ariadne. The stationary animals, trees and clouds contrast with these represented movements; but their outlines have a decorative rhythm of curves that echo the gestures and carry them lightly upward.

The representation of movement is not usually taken to be a distinctive value in Titian, but he was one of the few supreme, universal figures in art who combine almost every conceivable type of value, with such harmonious restraint that it is hard to single out any one. In his earlier work he often preserved the gentle tranquillity of Giorgione (for example, in the *Christ and Magdalen,* 270). Later, he tended to specialize on broad, simplified effects, anticipating the 17th century (for example, in the *Deposition* at Venice). *Bacchus and Ariadne* is one of the monumental works of his middle years, developing the early interest in movement that he had shown in the *Assumption* at Venice, but with all trace of the formal, symmetrical altar-piece gone. One must study the men who came before and after him to appreciate how well this picture assimilates the contributions of Raphael, Michelangelo and Giorgione, and anticipates the best in Rubens and Poussin. It is a crucial, high point in the long Greek and Renaissance effort to create an ideal of healthy, joyous and graceful humanity. The conception had ceased to be stiff, affected or monotonously and obviously rhythmic; it had been enriched by soft Venetian coloring; and it had not yet given way to Tintoretto's specialized interest in eccentric motion (compare his *St. George and the Dragon*, 16) or Veronese's in surface texture (*The Family of Darius before Alexander*, 294).

The coloring is now uneven in quality. The yellow and black of the leopards, and the blues of the sky and the central woman's dress are superficial and dislocated from their contexts, in a way that often results from retouching or deterioration (especially in the case of blue). They could hardly have been left so by the man who painted the deep, rich, realistic textures of Ariadne's head, and the cloth and vase in lower left. In an atmospheric Venetian picture, sharp-edged, superficial spots are jarring, whereas in the Uccello they are consistent with the whole. Aside from this weakness, color contributes to the total design a warm autumnal glow, and a pattern dancing with contrasts of scarlet, blue and purple against dull green and russet brown.

JAN VAN EYCK. JEAN ARNOLFINI AND HIS WIFE. (*Fig. 4; No. 186.*)

The distinctive value of this early Flemish work lies not in brilliant colors or in spirited action, but in the exquisite precision with which it handles small realistic details of light and texture, and the clarity with which it organizes them in deep space. Its charm is slow but increasing: one's eyes must adjust themselves to this different world of dignified repose and sombre shadows. The astonishing illusion of reality in some lighted parts may be first to attract attention: the way the chandelier hangs in empty space, with the exact lustre of old metal; the convex mirror focussing tiny reflections; the woman's head and fur sleeve; the sandals; the hands — all with microscopic details of surface visible. One feels the fine accuracy with which atmosphere is rendered: not rich, hazy or sparkling, but the

FIG. 4. JOHN ARNOLFINI AND HIS WIFE
By Van Eyck

cool, clear twilight of a north-country interior, shed through
space with infinitely subtle gradations.

Yet if this were all, the picture would be no more than
skilled mechanical copying of nature. It becomes art only
through selection, emphasis and organization. These qualities
become evident by contrast with inferior works in similar
vein — say the *Crucifixion* by the Master from Delft
(2922), or Crivelli's *Annunciation* (739), cluttered with
sharp linear details. Here it is only a few accented areas
that stand out in luminous, microscopic accuracy. Other,
broader surfaces of clothing, wall and floor are subordinated,
plain and dull. Even the man's face is modelled in comparatively broad, simplified planes. Thus the eye is led
unfailingly to follow the sequence of emphases, with large,
quiet, unconfusing stretches in between. These sequences
reward the eye in a decorative way by defining a simple,
balanced pattern of lines (including the chandelier above)
converging toward the clasped hands. Over it plays a soft
melody of rising and falling highlights, and beneath it
glows a dark harmony of reds and browns, half-realized
in the gray-green dusk.

EL GRECO. THE AGONY IN THE GARDEN. (*Fig. 5;
No. 3476.*)

Realism gives way to the opposite extreme in this fantastic
vision of a Spanish mystic. Figures and landscape are distorted, far removed from nature in shape, lighting, color
and texture. But unlike ordinary dream-pictures, it is organized, consistently directed to a purpose, not a mere
extravagant jumble. As representation, it gives clearly enough
the essentials of a story that was familiar and moving in the
intensely religious age of the Inquisition. But of greater interest now is the striking design of diagonal planes and

FIG. 5. THE AGONY IN THE GARDEN
By El Greco

vivid colors. In composition it is one of the latest of several different treatments of this theme, in which Greco sought more and more compression and simplification, the gathering together of scattered parts, the bringing out of main features with greater emphasis. In earlier versions, for example, the sleeping disciples were large, nearby and comparatively detached from the rest of the design. Here Christ and the angel are large and bold, in slashing angular strokes, while around them swirl twisting ovals of cloud. Smaller parts echo the diagonal swirling and crisscross motion of the larger ones. The painting is all in terms of pure color, not of light and line with color added on the surface. Again in contrast with the sombre Van Eyck, it flares with a lurid phosphorescent glow of changing colors, crimson, blue-green and golden yellow. Their clashing excitement is in harmony with the rhythm of movement, and with the general spirit of ecstatic drama.

Constable. The Haywain. (*Fig. 6; No. 1207.*)

Like Van Eyck's, Constable's art is one of quiet realism and solid, unostentatious craftsmanship. He succeeds in expressing the distinctive aspects of the English countryside, with all their associations of home and tranquillity. In so far as he pleases the eye directly, he does so by a peculiar diffused richness of color and light, rather than by any definite pattern. He follows the seventeenth century Dutch landscape painters in their formal, casual arrangements, emphasizing the freedom and easy, relaxed profusion of nature instead of reorganizing a scene into some artificially rhythmic design. What repetitions of shape do appear, such as those between the fluffy masses of clouds and trees, are never exact or conspicuous.

Yet the composition is not haphazard, a mere photograph

FIG. 6. THE HAYWAIN
By Constable

at random. One can best realize this by trying to imagine what would happen to the picture if various objects were shifted or omitted. A dog, a wagon, a house, a row of bushes, a plain and a row of trees — each is placed with care, to lead the eye by a series of light-accents into and around the scene, and to fill space adequately without confusion.

His most distinctive contribution is in color. To appreciate it, one may look at some typical Dutch landscape, such as Hobbema's *Woody Landscape* (995). There the general composition is similar, and the cool, dark, oily green and brown coloring. But the texture is more monotonous, with trees of a solid uniform green, varied only by touches of a lighter shade. The Constable is far more colorful, rich and luminous, with a soft iridescence that seems to penetrate deep into the inner substance of trees, grass and soil.

By looking at Rubens' *Chateau de Steen* (66) one can understand the general source of Constable's inspiration in this regard. The luminosity and richness which Hobbema lost is present in this earlier Flemish master. But there it is produced chiefly with broad strokes, thinly overpainted in various tints, and the whole landscape is given a more dramatic flare and swirl. The Constable is more quiet and static, with less flare and more sparkle, as a result of many dots and tiny streaks of red, yellow, brown and even blue, side by side among the prevailing green. This effect of "broken color," later developed and emphasized by Delacroix and the French impressionists, is in Constable rather subdued. He is not interested in brilliant, direct sunlight, or in bright decorative color; but in merging all parts of his landscape by soft transitions into one deep, continuous whole.

TURNER. ULYSSES DERIDING POLYPHEMUS. (*Fig. 7; No. 508.*)

Most of Turner's early works are superficial imitations of Claude Lorrain (see *Dido Building Carthage*, 498). His latest ones (such as *Queen Mab's Grotto*, 548) are highly specialized, abstract studies of light and color, anticipating Monet not only in brilliance but in a tendency to weaken design by melting away all definite shapes and positions in space. His light and color, so completely deprived of form, often degenerate into mere flashy smears of paint. The works of his middle years, the *Ulysses* and the *Fighting Temeraire* (524), combine originality with comparative strength of organization.

Never before or since has the splendor of the sun, rising or setting over water, been preserved with such magnificence and realism. The soft, gentle glow of Claude is raised to an explosion of red and gold that sets the sky and sea ablaze. The classical tradition, handed down through Claude, survives in the portrayal of these Greek galleys, but with more of the epic vigor, the "surge and thunder" of its subject, the Odyssey, than any previous painter had expressed. There is a debt to Rubens, too, in this dramatic excitement, this love for turbulent contrasts of cloud and sunshine, but the total effect is to be found in no earlier work of art. Brilliant as they are, the colors of this middle period are restrained from becoming mere daubs of paint by orderly gradations of light and shadow. Objects recede in space, and they build up definite rhythms of three-dimensional shape: for example, the fan-like diverging of masts, oars and rays of light; the curving planes of the rocks and clouds, and of the prows and sails of the ships.

These interrelations of shape are not carried far enough to organize the picture into a definite design; by comparison

FIG. 7. ULYSSES DERIDING POLYPHEMUS
By Turner

with a Claude or a Cézanne, the picture is loose and vague. But it is organized in terms of atmosphere to exactly the extent intended, and there is no sense of inconsistency or falling apart. The subject is a misty sunrise, and a certain haziness is suitable. If its rather grandiose, melodramatic glamor seems exaggerated in the present age, that quality is thoroughly characteristic of the age in which it was painted: the close of the romantic period.

Briefer Mention

Italian: A. DAL CASTAGNO, *Crucifixion* (1138) — spaciousness; rugged strength of modelling; dramatic intensity of emotion. PIERO DELLA FRANCESCA, *Baptism* (665) — stately, simple dignity of drawing; spaciousness; color contrast; faded but still luminous blue-gray atmosphere. PISANELLO, *Vision of St. Eustace* (1436) — tapestry-like design of light-colored animals, naturally represented but thrown in distorted perspective against dark wooded landscape. GIOVANNI BELLINI, *Death of St. Peter Martyr* (812) — landscape made realistic through subtle blending of light and color, to give deep, soft, organic textures and continuous, diffused atmosphere. TINTORETTO, *Vincenzo Morosini* (4004) — weary old age expressed in drooping, swaying rhythm of lines and shadows that hollow, twist and elongate features; cloth-folds also long, drooping, emphatic, with streaks of light and rich color. TIEPOLO, *Deposition* (1333) — a dashing, dramatic and firmly built design in broad, simplified strokes of light and color, anticipating Daumier and Goya.

Dutch and Flemish: HOBBEMA, *The Avenue, Middelharnis* (830) — a striking design of converging perspectives and tree-plumes against clouds; saved from over-regularity by line-variations in tree-trunks and color-contrasts in sec-

tions of land. DE HOOCH, *Courtyard of a Dutch House*
(794) — an apparently casual backyard scene, strongly organized by arrangement of planes in space, color-contrasts
and fine sunlight gradations. RUBENS, *Judgment of Paris*
(194) — Rubens at his best, in rich Venetian coloring and
vigorous but not exaggerated swirling rhythm of robust
bodies.

Spanish, German and British: VELAZQUEZ, *Venus*
(2057) — a realistic nude (unusual subject for him) given
unified design by converging of long, sweeping, deeply indented curves, contrasted and blended fresh clear reds and
grays, and flattened abbreviation of unaccented parts.
HOLBEIN, *The Ambassadors* (1314) — minutely photographic representation; a balanced, elaborate design of
planes in shallow space; coloring hard, superficial; lacks
emphasis. CROME, *The Poringland Oak* (2674) — Dutch
realism with a new, quietly luminous English atmosphere,
less sparkling than Constable's. HOGARTH, *Calais Gate*
(1464) — terse, lively comic illustration.

The Wallace Collection

The special treasure here is one of REMBRANDT's greatest pictures, *The Centurion Cornelius*, or *The Unmerciful
Servant*. Lacking the complex deep-space design of *The
Night Watch*, it achieves more concentrated force through
the sombrely majestic reds and golds that flame suddenly
out of enveloping darkness, placing four figures among the
shadows with magical reality, and bringing out a fitful play
of lights and textures, together with a tense emotional
drama in the four expressive, opposing faces. Less subtle
but more vivacious is *The Laughing Cavalier* of FRANS
HALS, in slashing, bold strokes and ornate coloring consistent with the gay good humor it expresses. VELAZQUEZ

FIG. 8. THE SWING
By Fragonard

has a deftly simplified portrait, *The Lady with the Fan,*
in his own delicately blended blacks and silver-blues, surrounding creamy flesh-tints that make the Hals look wooden.
Many of the numerous eighteenth century French are
second-rate, including all the Bouchers and some of the
larger canvases by WATTEAU. His small *Music Lesson*
(377) and *Gilles and his Family* (381), in Room XVIII,
have more delicately fragile, iridescent surfaces, and more
spontaneous, unconventional drawing.

FRAGONARD. THE SWING. (*Fig. 8; No. 430.*)

The spirit of eighteenth century French court painting,
and the taste of the aristocratic society that supported it, are
well represented by this bit of pretty decoration. Too often
the art of this period was stereotyped, over-loaded with dead,
conventional surface ornament, as in most of the examples
in this collection. Especially, as in the Bouchers here, it
tended to become a mere weak, plastery echo of the classical
Renaissance. But occasionally it expressed the ideals of its
age in a fresh, consistent way, and the result is a distinctive
world of the imagination. Simplicity and strength are not
features of that world, nor an honest look at ugliness and
tragedy; it is a dream of endless luxury and gay amusements.

The rhythm of motion in this picture, appropriately, is
one of light, dainty, fluttery swirls, in silken flounces tossed
coquettishly, and in the twisting flight of branches overhead.
The countless small details are well organized and subordinated in large groupings. Color and light are neither
too strong and rich for the purpose, nor insensitively hard
and superficial. They create a deep space and a kind of
substance that are quite unnatural, but convincing enough
in their own way. Nothing is firm, plain or solid; everything floats in a delicate mist of soft green foliage, thornless

FIG. 9. BATHERS
By Seurat

roses, pink and lavender silks and fluffy pale blue clouds. There is obviously nothing in it to move one deeply, but within its limits it is successful as a harmonious, original and fairly complex design.

The National Gallery at Millbank

This building is devoted largely to recent and contemporary art, and often some of its best exhibits are temporary loans. Among the permanent ones, the most famous are the many landscapes by TURNER. Most of the larger ones show him unsuccessfully trying to imitate Claude Lorrain; but *The Burial at Sea* (528) is in his more original, impressionistic style. Gainsborough, Romney, Reynolds, Rossetti, Watts, Burne-Jones and Sargent attract popular taste; Constable, Blake and Bonington the more discriminating. WHISTLER's misty twilights and Japanese-inspired compositions are slight but distinctive. Among the French, these are notable: DAUMIER's *Don Quixote* and *Troisième Classe;* MANET's *Servante de Bocks;* RENOIR's *Parapluies, La Première Sortie* and *Nu dans l'eau;* CÉZANNE's *Self-portrait* and *Aix, paysage rocheux;* GAUGUIN's *Faa Iheihe* and VAN GOGH's *Yellow Chair.*

SEURAT. THE BATHERS. (*Fig. 9.*)

In many works of the impressionist movement, brilliancy and iridescence of coloring were emphasized to such an extent that all strength of design was lost. Objects had no definite shapes; their arrangement in space was vague and misty. Seurat, along with Cézanne and Renoir, succeeded in organizing the new brilliant color and light into firm, rhythmic designs of solid objects in deep space, thus restoring to painting some of the old values of Renaissance art,

FIG. 10. SATAN SMITING JOB

By Blake

along with the new ones of impressionism. This is one of
the few late, elaborately developed works of the short-lived
Seurat; most of the pictures bearing his name are slight
sketches or early, purely impressionist studies. He employs in
it the peculiar technique called "pointillism" or "neo-
impressionism," consisting of rather large, similarly shaped
dots of contrasting color side by side, the colors being
chosen and arranged with mathematical care so as to blend
into the desired sparkling tints. The picture's value, however, lies not in this mechanical technique, now obsolete,
but in the design he achieved with it or in spite of it. There
is a monumental quality, as of Egyptian sculpture, in these
immense rigid figures placed immovably at definite intervals
in space, welded together by insistent repetition of the same
short curves (in the boys' backs, heads, hats and shoes, and
in the distant sail-boats). They stand out with unnatural,
striking clarity and dazzling richness of color, every shadow
as well as every highlight throbbing with some intense violet,
green or blue unknown to pre-impressionist painting.

WILLIAM BLAKE. SATAN SMITING JOB. (*Fig. 10; No.
3340.*)

The strange art of Blake can be adequately understood
only through studying his drawings and water-colors in
relation to his poetic dramas. It is not a purely pictorial art,
but one relying heavily on literary, religious and other associated values. His pictures depend almost wholly on line
drawing for their effects; color is often omitted, and is at
best a thin, decorative wash between sharp lines. In spite
of these limitations, and largely because of the unique, weird
fascination of the dream-world they represent, Blake's pictures have attained a rank in art far higher than those of his
contemporaries, Gainsborough, Reynolds and Romney,

whose facile use of paint expresses only trivial imaginings. He is deeply indebted to Michelangelo, not only for his rhythmic designs of muscular bodies, but for their power to express the majestic grandeur of the Old Testament and of Dante's mystical visions. On this basis he develops qualities of line that are all his own. One is a power of suggestive illustration: the ability to convey with a few terse lines the essentials of some tremendous epic vision.

In *Satan Smiting Job,* every detail coöperates to suggest the swooping of fiery wings, the emptying of the vials of wrath, the writhing of Job's torment, and the drooping figure of hopeless pity at his feet. A lurid sunset, with alternate scalloped rings of light and dark, mauve, blue and rose above dull yellow earth, adds a background suitably fantastic and explosive. The rhythms of line are full of contrast: sometimes dramatically sweeping; sometimes tense, suppressed and cramped; sometimes rippling and twisting in long flowing streams, as in Job's hair and beard, and in the flaming liquid pouring down. Natural proportions are freely altered, in the building up of some bizarre design of contorted, huddled, or flying, wind-swept bodies. Thus his scanty technical resources are used with such hypnotic power to stimulate the imagination, that one almost forgets the slightness of what is actually offered to the eye.

The British Museum

Sculpture and ethnological exhibits fill most of the British Museum, but some excellent pictures are also tucked away at odd corners in its depths. The *Grenville Library,* on the right of the entrance hall, shows under glass a changing exhibit of MEDIEVAL ILLUMINATED MANUSCRIPTS, with bizarrely decorative, strongly rhythmic drawings and flat color-patterns in great variety of national and individual

styles. Most distinctive are the English works, especially the
eleventh century *Gospels*, the twelfth century *Life of St.
Guthlac*, and a *Psalter*, *Apocalypse*, *Missal* and *Hours of
the Virgin* of later dates. GREEK VASE DRAWINGS are
shown on the upper floor, at left, especially in the Second
and Third Vase Rooms. The art appears at its height in the
Athenian black-figured vases of the sixth century B.C., and
in the red-figured vases labelled " Transition from Severe to
Fine Style " and " Finest Style." Especially notable are
the drawings by SOTADES on white surfaces, and the large
Combat of Amazons and Heroes.

On the second floor of *King Edward VII's Gallery* is a
changing exhibit of drawings and etchings by REMBRANDT,
BLAKE and others, and of PERSIAN AND INDIAN MINIA-
TURES, CHINESE AND JAPANESE PAINTINGS AND PRINTS.
Some typical examples of these oriental paintings are discussed in the following pages. Other Chinese pictures of
importance are the *Admonitions of the Instructress in the
Palace*, by KU K'AI CHIH, of the fourth century A.D., delicate and sophisticated in line drawing; the magnificent large
fresco of *Three Bodhisattvas*; the Sung dynasty *Lotus and
White Heron*. The Japanese SESSHU is represented by *Hotei
and Children*; MATABEI by two *Dancers*.

EGYPTIAN (15TH CENTURY B.C.). MUSIC AND DANC-
ING AT A BANQUET. (*Fig. 11; 4th Egyptian Room.*)

This fragment of a Theban wall-painting is characteristic
in several ways of ancient Egyptian painting in general. In
particular, it is notable for its flatness, for its prevailingly uniform, stiff linear rhythm, and for its crude, bright color-
pattern. Within this narrow range, it achieves a simple,
obvious, but forceful decorative quality. Its boldly contrasting spots of blue, several tints of red, black and white, in a

FIG. 11. MUSIC AND DANCING AT A BANQUET

Egyptian

dry, chalky tempera surface, are confined within sharp firm outlines, except where one film is spread thinly over another to represent transparent clothing. There is no hint of shading or modelling, or of depth, except through the overlapping of one limb by another. The guests in the upper row are drawn (as usual with noble or divine personages) in a conventionally artificial style, of rigid arcs and angles in unvarying succession. Their faces and legs are in profile; their shoulders, and one large eye in each head, are drawn as if seen from the front. The girl musicians and dancers below are drawn with unusually informal realism, two of them full-face, with relaxed and supple outlines that sway and intertwine in a lively dance rhythm.

Mu Ch'i (Chinese, Sung Period). Tiger. (*Fig. 12*.)

Chinese painting of the Sung dynasty, when it reached its highest development, is subtle and suggestive; never obvious or elaborate. It is neither abstract decoration nor a literal imitation of nature, but, as always in the greatest painting, a combination of realism with design. Once its peculiar idioms have been grasped, it will be found to speak the universal, basic language of pictorial form. Its means are simple: principally line, and various shades of light and dark; color contributes little. With these means the painter seeks, not only to present a rhythm of repeated themes, but to put down what seem to him the few essential, distinctive qualities of the natural objects he is painting — these and no more.

What are the essential qualities of the reeds that grow beside a stream? They have a distinctive slender stiffness; their leaves stick out in dark, spear-like points; the wind blows them in a certain way; they break off and lie on the

FIG. 12. TIGER
By Mu Ch'i

ground in a certain way. To grasp this and be able to put it down vividly with the fewest possible strokes of the brush, one must observe these reeds for days and years, and practise drawing them until every stroke counts to the utmost. The same with a tiger: how does he turn and glare through the forest? How does his fur take the light, as the fur of no other animal does? These are problems, not of copying, but of revealing and interpreting nature. Then, in addition, the fascination of repeated forms in nature, of subtle, concealed resemblances between things otherwise very different, impels the painter to put them together in a design. The reed-leaves are like the tiger's stripes, but more distinct. They stand, as he does, tense and alert, with diagonal outlines crossing each other. His left shoulder curves as does the swaying branch overhead, and so does the distant waterfall. The leaves overhead make a soft mottled silhouette against the light, that resembles the soft shadowing of his fur. Of such elements, woven together, a new design is created. The painter would scorn to copy every shadow cast in an actual scene, or imitate perspective lines. He can suggest solidity (as in the tiger's muscular leg) or deep space (as in the waterfall) without actually copying them.

CHINESE (MING DYNASTY, UNKNOWN PAINTER). THE EARTHLY PARADISE. (*Fig. 13.*)

In this period Chinese painting began to lose the austere simplicity and force of the Sung Dynasty, and to begin its long descent into loose over-decoration and literal detail. Here this tendency has not yet gone unpleasantly far. The composition is full of small details, diffusely scattered, with no tightly knit pattern. But the effect is not one of confusion: rather of delicate, free-floating, gossamer lightness.

FIG. 13. THE EARTHLY PARADISE
Chinese, Ming Dynasty

This unifying spirit is conveyed in the swaying, willowy outlines of the ladies; in the intricate, fine-spun swirls of their
drapery; in the sinuous, long-necked cranes; in the falling
flower-petals, the gently rippling waves, and in the wandering, cloudy shapes of trees and hills. The mood expressed
in faces and attitudes is, consistently, one of gay, thoughtless pleasure, tea-drinking, boating and gathering flowers.
Between the figures and their background there is a contrast in light and color so great as to prevent any near approach to realistic space or atmosphere. The former stand
out in isolation as flat, ornate little patterns of intricate line
and bright varied color. The landscape is in quite another
key, of dull gray-greens in carefully varied shades. But the
same flow of line links both together, and the dark smudges
of the trees provide a good decorative counterfoil to the
bright little figures. There is a much more pronounced illusion of deep space than in the nearby T'ang paintings by
Ku K'ai Chih. But all spatial intervals, and the relative sizes
of things, are vague and unrealistic. With no attempt at
anything more substantial, the picture achieves a distinctive,
harmonious charm, not unlike that of Fragonard's *The
Swing*. (*Fig. 8.*)

HOKUSAI (JAPANESE). RATS AND CAPSICUM PODS. (*Fig. 14.*)

To be good art, a picture does not have to be exalted in
subject or complex in structure. One of the hardest tests of
the painter's art is to take an utterly trivial subject such as
this, and in a few strokes produce a form that holds our
interest. True, it lacks richness of color, intricate pattern,
solidity, depth, and many other values that painting can
possess. It is no greater than thousands of other sketches
and prints that flowed from the quick, observant brush of

FIG. 14. RATS AND CAPSICUM PODS

By Hokusai

Hokusai. But it is included here as an example of extreme economy and terseness: qualities of high value in such arts as drawing and etching, where the medium itself limits the form, and where brief suggestiveness rather than full elaboration is appropriate. Every stroke of the ink-brush in this sketch is effective in two ways. First, as representation, it conveys a vivid sense of the shape and light, agile posture that are characteristic of these little animals. As decoration, it presents with simple force an observed rhythm in nature, an essential resemblance between rats and seed-pods: both slender, irregularly bent, with long, thread-like whiskers, tails and stems. By deft gradations in the shade of gray, and by varied outlines — sometimes sharp, sometimes ragged — it achieves a spontaneous, living quality as decoration that is lacking in the Utamaro print. At the same time it suggests the velvety, ragged fur and ears of the rats, and the wiriness of their claws and whiskers. The debt to Sung art is obvious, but it does not amount to imitation. The Japanese form is slighter, but livelier.

UTAMARO. A GIRL AND HER REFLECTION. (*Fig. 15.*)

This print represents one of the more decorative types of Japanese pictorial art. It is, first of all, an intricate linear arabesque of flowing, interlacing curves and loops. Some of these lines serve to mark off areas differing in light-and-dark value. Each area has some definite, uniform degree of lightness; there are no soft gradual transitions from one to another. Step by step, they form a series of shades, from the jet blackness of the hair, mirror-frame and table, to the paper-whiteness of the faces. They are placed, not to represent the natural falling of highlights and shadows, but to form a pattern, in which each particular shade is a theme to be repeated in various shapes and sizes. The areas are

FIG. 15. A GIRL AND HER REFLECTION
By Utamaro

contrasted also in color and texture: besides black and white, some are plain yellow or green, some flowered red or violet. Aside from their contribution to the pattern of contrasts, the colors have little surface charm. Being merely diluted washes of uniform thinness on paper, they lack the richness, intensity and subtlety of other media. Japanese prints, like other exotic, non-realistic forms, have exerted a refreshing influence on modern European art, helping to free it from its own conventions. But in comparison with the great Chinese and Japanese painting from which they are descended, they represent a decline in creative vigor. The quality of line in this picture, for example, is rather monotonous, hard and insensitive, and the pattern it weaves is tightly crystallized, academically formal, rather than free and spontaneous.

PERSIAN (TIMURID PERIOD, LATE 15TH CENTURY). THE MINISTERS OF HORMUZD PLEAD WITH HIM FOR HIS SON. (*Fig. 16; From a manuscript, Or. 6810, f 37.*)

Byzantine, North Indian and Chinese influences combined with native Persian genius to produce a distinctive art of miniature painting, which flourished from the 14th to the 18th century. The earlier works show, on the whole, more freedom and animation in line drawing; the later ones more decorative treatment of surfaces, which finally become overloaded with stereotyped ornamental detail.

In the example shown the style is still both restrained and spontaneous. Beside its quaint illustrative interest, it has a vivacious pattern of lines and colors. The colors are quite superficial, without tinting or shading; but these very limitations are necessary to produce the vivid, jewel-like intensity with which each separate part gleams out in pure vermilion, turquoise, lapis lazuli, emerald or coral. If they were

FIG. 16. THE MINISTERS OF HORMUZD
PLEADING FOR HIS SON
Persian

separated by soft, melting Venetian transitions, instead of by knife-edge outlines, they would not produce such a lively play of sudden contrasts.

The whole picture is divided into contrasting sections. Around the human figures, the background is cut into many parallelograms and strips of different size, some in plain solid colors, gold or black, others covered with fine intricate floral, geometrical or calligraphic ornamentation, in the same bright colors and gold. Against the flat blue sky, jewel-like flowers and bending trees are silhouetted. The linear outlines of each section, including the human figures, are usually quite simple, repeating some obvious theme of curve or angle. But the effect of all the sections fitted together, usually in unsymmetrical, surprising ways, is complex and richly decorative.

The natural converging of lines in perspective is distorted with the utmost freedom. It cannot be said that the picture is entirely flat, for approximate perspectives and recessions in space are suggested (as in the couch, gate and house). But the lines are placed, not where they would naturally fall, but where the pattern calls for them. The more distant objects, instead of being placed behind the nearer ones, are pushed upward, toward the top of the picture. Each individual man is seen as if from the same level with him; but the tiled floor, carpet or ground beneath him is seen as if tilted up edgewise, or looked down on from above. The figures, near and far, are scattered over it with equal relative size and clarity, to make them equally effective as parts of the design.

INDIAN (MUGHAL SCHOOL, 18TH CENTURY). SCENE FROM A ROMANCE. (*Fig. 17.*)

Among the oriental forms of art which are winning a larger place in western museums are the Mughal and Rajput schools of miniature painting. The art of painting was revived in India by the Mughal or Mogul emperors in the 16th century, at first under strong Persian influence. In the more fully developed style of the Mughal school the Persian element has diminished, and a European interest in deep space, modelling and realistic atmosphere — here that of moonlight and torchlight — has taken its place. At the same time the style has come nearer to the native Hindu tradition of line drawing, which was relaxed and flowing although strongly rhythmic. There is less brilliant surface decoration than in the Persian miniature just discussed; more interest in representing human faces, animals, birds and plants.

This picture is characteristic in that human figures and horses are rendered in bright surface colors and gold, only slightly shaded, while the background is of dark, dull landscape greens and browns, deep and shadowy. The result, as in *The Earthly Paradise*, is an extreme contrast between the two parts of the picture, amounting to lack of perfect unity. The case is similar also to that of Gentile da Fabriano, who tried to combine the Byzantine and Renaissance styles. Here the inconsistency is lessened by the fact that both figures and background are drawn in highly stylized, non-realistic lines. The background recalls both Chinese and Byzantine landscape (see Fig. 66) in its rhythmic flow of clearly outlined rocky points and crevices, almost flat, and bordered with mossy tufts of foliage equally flat. The shadows are broadly suffused, and do not round out individual objects. The curves of the horses and riders are

FIG. 17. SCENE FROM A ROMANCE
Indian (Mughal)

distinctly continued and repeated in the background, which further integrates the picture as a surface pattern. The technique is precise and sure throughout. This type of art makes no claim to accurate realism, and its slight step in that direction, if preventing a decorative brilliance equal to the Persian, adds the different charm of a delicate, fantastically poetic view of nature.

Other Galleries

The *Victoria and Albert Museum* at South Kensington contains some spirited sketches in oils by CONSTABLE, and some late RAPHAEL tapestry-cartoons. In its Indian Section, on the Imperial Institute Road, are Indian MUGHAL manuscript paintings, LAMAIST monastery paintings from Thibet, and fresco copies of Buddhist cave-paintings at Ajanta. Less important are the *Dulwich Gallery*, with a second-rate REMBRANDT *Girl at a Window*, and the *Burlington House*, with many academic moderns, a good CONSTABLE *Leaping Horse* and some LEONARDO drawings.

CHAPTER II

FRANCE

PARIS

FOR three centuries, the city of Paris has been the world's artistic capital. There, as in no other city, the making of pictures is still a vital public interest: a career and a business with some, and a hobby with many others. Interest in art, and some appreciation of it, are diffused to a surprising extent through the masses. Painters go to the Louvre to study, and back to their studios to paint. A good share of that museum is filled with the works of past residents of Paris, French and foreign, and every generation contributes or hopes to contribute to it. The works of past ages are there, but as parts of one continuous tradition leading down to the present, and helping to shape the future.

This busy atmosphere does much to dispel the tomb-like deadness, the air of a long-vanished past, which hangs about most other art museums. Newcomers who absorb a little of this atmosphere usually find their attitude toward art becoming less condescending, or less vaguely respectful, as the case may be, and more keenly interested, more understanding and critical. It can best be felt by visiting not only the Louvre but the Luxembourg Museum, where recent work is shown, the various *Salons*, academic and radical, and some of the small current exhibits in shops along the Rue la Boëtie.

The Louvre

In the Louvre, it can best be felt by paying special attention to the rooms of late nineteenth century art, which are in remote parts of the building, and are missed entirely by the stream of ordinary tourists. These are the *Camondo Collection* and the recently opened *Salle Caillebotte*. In relation to these, one can study French art of the early nineteenth century in Salle VIII, and of previous centuries in Salles I (*La Caze*) and X to XVI. Magnificent as the Italian and other foreign rooms are, they are paralleled elsewhere, and the traveller who is going on to other countries would be wise not to spend all his time there.

The Louvre as a whole is undoubtedly the most important as well as the largest art museum in the world, and the most rewarding to long exploration. At the same time, its superlative size and richness make it the hardest of all museums in which to find one's way about, and in which to discover the best. For the Louvre has much that is mediocre or worse; it has not been pruned down with so rigorous a hand as have many smaller galleries. Here the mediocre too often obscures the best, by its conspicuousness and quantity. Small, delicate jewels of painting are lost on enormous crowded walls. Masterpieces that mark epochs in art history are hidden up stairways and around corners in little side rooms, to be reached only by interminable passageways cluttered with miscellaneous exhibits. The casual visitor, with a limited time to spend, could by no possible chance discover them without guidance. So vast is each wing that many visitors wander for hours in a single group of rooms, perhaps seeing only the French, or only the Italian paintings, then depart unaware that they have missed nine tenths of the important pictures of the Louvre. To go straight through the museum, from room to room and floor to floor, looking at everything on the way with equal attention, is nothing short of deadly. In the Louvre if nowhere else, one should decide in advance what to see first, and go directly to it. Then, after enjoying the few works of outstanding importance in a leisurely way, one can afford to roam about more aimlessly for the added pleasure of unexpected discoveries.

What is best in the Louvre? No two writers will agree exactly. But there are a few unique, world-famous pictures which, almost every critic will agree, should not be missed. What artists, and what schools of painting, are best represented here? First of all, as suggested above, is the French tradition, from the fifteenth century to the twentieth. For the last two centuries, at least, France has led the way in the art of painting, and thus a generous proportion of the highest achievements of modern art are here. Of the seventeenth century, when productive genius flamed up intensely in France, Holland, Flanders and Spain, only the last school is poorly represented; for that one must go to Madrid itself. Of the other three, the Louvre has some worthy examples, along with much that does no credit to great names. Here, too, one can see the Renaissance in its Flemish, French and German phases. Of the Italian phase, the inspiration of all the others, the fourteenth and early fifteenth centuries are not shown at their best, which is often in fresco and untransportable. But the late Renaissance, Florentine and Venetian, is here in all its grandeur of statuesque modelling, monumental design and idealized humanity. Unfortunately, its colors are too often dimmed in the Louvre by murky brown films of grime and varnish, which an over-cautious administration hesitates to remove.

Many of the chief Renaissance masters, though well represented here, have as good or better works elsewhere. One only, LEONARDO DA VINCI, can be studied better here than in any other museum. His famous picture of *Mona Lisa* is not only the most famous portrait in the world, and the first objective of most visitors to the Louvre; it presents a complex and difficult problem for critical appraisal. On the one hand, it is exalted in poetic rhapsodies as the world's greatest picture; on the other, it is denounced as a piece of sentimental trickery, lacking in all genuine artistic value.

LEONARDO DA VINCI. MONA LISA (LA JOCONDE). (*Fig. 18; in Salle C, near center of the Grande Galerie.*)

The unequalled fame of this portrait rests almost wholly upon one particular kind of appeal: on the expression of a face, and its power to suggest a mysterious personality behind it. The immediate effect, for most observers, is an impulse to interpret that expression in terms of some familiar emotion or type of character. Is it a mood of disillusioned irony, one asks, in which Mona Lisa looks out upon the world? Is it weariness, gentle mockery, condescending aloofness or pitying tenderness that one reads behind that mask of suave control? Thus the observer is tempted to dream romantic mysteries about an imagined woman, while, too often, his eyes pay little heed to the actual picture before him.

Nevertheless, there is something actually here that has power to stimulate such fancies. There is a pictured face, with shadows cunningly arranged to represent slight peculiarities in the shape and tension of the features. Their sug-

FIG. 18. MONA LISA
By Leonardo da Vinci

gestive power is due in part to brushwork of exquisite subtlety, that could set down unerringly the minutest intended
gradations of light and shadow. (Copyists find them almost
impossible to reproduce, and the slightest change makes the
whole face a caricature.) In addition, that skill was guided
by profound knowledge of facial expressions and what they
signify, based at once on a sensitive feeling for the nuances
of human personality and on keen observation of their slight,
momentary signs. In his *Last Supper* at Milan, Leonardo
constructed a whole drama of contrasting personalities, by
means of expressive faces and gestures. Here in the Mona
Lisa, the peculiarities of feature which he has assembled are
more or less like some which we have seen elsewhere —
otherwise they would have no meaning to us — but we
have never seen them in this exact combination. It is not an
ordinary combination; it suggests no familiar, simple emotion, as the faces of Fra Angelico do, but rather several at
once, that do not commonly go together. It suggests them
all rather indefinitely, as in a face where inward feeling is
half concealed by sophisticated reserve, or where several
half-realized thoughts and fancies together share the mind,
and hold it in vague musing contemplation.

In real life we might fail to notice such an expression; it
would vanish in a moment, and even while it lasted other
things would be competing for our attention. But here nothing competes; the expression is arrested, emphasized. Significant details, such as faint shadows about the eyes and mouth,
are put down with the finest precision. Elsewhere, as in the
hair and darker portions of the dress, the painting is simpler,
less emphatic. A clear light, strongly focussed but not glaring, brings the face into distinct sculptural relief. It accents
nothing else but the hands, which likewise express a suave,
controlled, inactive personality. There are no exaggerated,
melting shadows; Leonardo resorts here to no obvious

theatrical trick, as he does in *St. John the Baptist* (42), to
give an air of mystery. The picture relies simply and straight-
forwardly on the human interest of the represented face.

It is not displeasing as a purely decorative form, apart
from this interest. The modelling has the same direct sensuous charm as the late Greek sculpture which inspired it: the
charm of smooth old marble, delicately shaped to take soft,
changing highlights and shadows. There is even a hint of
design in the way the slight upturning of the lips is repeated,
unobtrusively, at the corners of the eyes, and again in the
shadows of cheeks and chin. The hands droop downward,
reversing the curve. This imparts a quiet undulation which
continues in the curves of hair and dress, and in the winding road and river. The coloring is not rich or deep, and the
flesh tints have faded from their former crimson to a dead
greenish ivory, with only a tinge of rose in the hands. Hair
of deep reddish brown, a dress of brown and green, (fairly
soft and cloth-like by comparison with other pictures of the
time) and a fantastic landscape of russet and pale olive, rising to a phosphorescent sea-green in the sky, frame the dull
ivory face in a sombre color-harmony.

These decorative aspects are pleasing, but provide no
claim to greatness. The picture stands or falls as a piece of
characterization in paint; and as such it ranks in force and
interest with the most memorable characters of literature.
That appeal is too indirect and specialized, however, to
make the picture deeply satisfying to persons who have
learned to enjoy the many direct values of design.

GIORGIONE. A CONCERT IN THE OPEN AIR (LE CON-
CERT CHAMPÊTRE). (*Fig. 19; No. 1136.*)

Unlike the Mona Lisa, this picture appeals in many different ways: not only through the human associations of its

subject-matter, but more directly through its complex, finely organized design. Unlike Titian's *Bacchus and Ariadne*, it involves no representation of bodily movement. What movement it has is of the decorative sort: that is, an inter-relation of parts which the sensitive observer feels as rhythmic repetition, flow and opposition. Like the Titian, again, it is infused with rich Venetian color; and its composition is relaxed, unsymmetrical, irregular, to an extent that suggests Titian rather than Bellini, late rather than early Venetian painting. The men's figures, in particular, are drawn with a vigorous naturalism that resembles the work of Titian rather than the definitely known work of Giorgione. Titian is known to have completed several unfinished works of Giorgione, and that may well have been the case here. But the suave, gentle modelling of the two women, and the air of tranquillity that pervades the landscape, are qualities essentially Giorgionesque. Some relatively dead, superficial areas (the lute and the hand playing it, and the nearby green slope just to the left) seem to reveal the work of a late retoucher much less skilled than either.

As a whole, the picture retains a deep organic color at-mosphere which is impressive by contrast with the Raphaels and Leonardos in the room. All through the spacious scene, deep autumnal browns, greens and golds melt into one another, rising to a lustrous climax in the center and focus of the whole composition, the crimson sleeve of the lute-player. Repetitions of shape further knit the design together: every line of the human figures, the hillside slopes, the tops and branches of the trees, fits into the pattern of diagonals, parallel and intersecting, crescent-shaped or flattened, with a few contrasting verticals in the well, tree-trunk and distant houses. All these repetitions are so irregular and subtle as never to obtrude themselves with artificial formality. Most of the lines which form them are dissolved into gentle

FIG. 19. A CONCERT IN THE OPEN AIR

By Giorgione

shadows, so that one is conscious not of outlines, but of softly rounded masses, some bending almost in unison, some bending gracefully toward each other, some floating backward into space. The same rich-textured fullness defines nude bodies, garments, trees, hills and clouds. In short, all the principal values of Renaissance painting, save that of strenuous bodily movement, are combined with an easy maturity that conceals all technical framework. Expressed through the formal design, and humanizing it, is the Arcadian spirit of Theocritus and Virgil: the peaceful serenity of a golden late summer afternoon, and of people whose manner of life combines pastoral simplicity with cultivated elegance and grace.

TITIAN. THE MAN WITH THE GLOVE. (*Fig. 20; No. 1592.*)

The variety of possible aims and values in portraiture is evident if one compares the four or five great examples that are close together in the *Grande Galerie*. The *Mona Lisa*, as we have seen, is notable for psychological representation of a more or less idealized, imaginative type. Farther down is Rembrandt's *Portrait of Himself as an Old Man* (2555), also penetrating and subtle in character-portrayal, with profounder realism, modelling less sculptural, and a mastery of dull half-lights and melting shadows. Tintoretto's *Portrait of Himself* (1466) also as an old man, reveals that intense, agitated personality by means of deep, grooving shadows, that distort the face and beard into a throbbing flow of curves. Raphael's *Balthasar Castiglione* (1505) is, like its painter, less profound psychologically, more bland and superficial; but it shows a vigorous, unsentimental realism, and a mastery of delicate gray tones, which raise it above his early works.

FIG. 20. THE MAN WITH THE GLOVE
By Titian

None of these portraits has the direct visual appeal, as rich color and striking pattern, that is evident in *The Man with the Glove*. The type of mind behind the face is clearly enough expressed: it is neither bland, subtly tortuous, nor agitated, but direct, alert and self-controlled. But these associations are not forced upon the observer, or conveyed merely by facial expression. They are implicit in the design itself, which is a simple, firm one, of three long straight triangles brought almost to a focus: the head and shirt front, the left hand with pointed finger, the right hand with two gloves. They stand out in clear illumination against a plain dark background, supported by a broader pattern of long, straight diagonals, defined by shoulders, hair and coat-folds. Minor details — the straight nose, the fingers, small partings in the hair, collar and gloves — fit subtly into this rhythm of slender angles. The right hand is a supreme example of deep, organic color used to model a solid, living object. Its warm flesh tints, deftly blended with gray-green shadows, not only give a vivid sense of the essential structure of a human hand, and of the quiet, relaxed power in this particular hand; they also create a new plastic form, directly satisfying in itself, over and above what it represents, as a strongly modelled shape composed of rich and sombrely luminous color.

MANTEGNA. CALVARY. (*Fig. 21; No. 1373.*)

The distinctive element here is the use of long, sharp, flowing lines. Their basic structure is firm: tall verticals against intersecting, receding diagonals. Over them the small details engrave a winding scroll-work of unnatural clarity, emphasized by long linear streaks of light. Later Venetian painting softened such lines with richer color and melted them into plainer masses. The direct effect on the

FIG. 21. CALVARY
By Mantegna

eye is somewhat edgy, acrid, cramped, ungrateful. But such qualities are more consistent with the pain, the agony and pity represented than are the suavity and sensuous richness found in later treatments of the same subject, when religious emotion had become less deeply sincere. And there is a certain decorative beauty, essentially Gothic, in this intricate music of line. It is enhanced by other, newer elements: a statuesque dignity borrowed from Roman sculpture, in the attitudes and draperies, the solid anatomical modelling, and the deep perspectives of the Florentine Renaissance.

LORENZO LOTTO. SAINT JEROME IN THE DESERT. (*Fig. 22; No. 1350.*)

Small and inconspicuous, this work of a minor Venetian is surprisingly modern in its treatment of landscape. The fresh, cool, mossy texture of the rocks anticipates Courbet. Their massive simplification, and their zig-zag, piling-up recession in space, with the human figure small and fitted unobtrusively in, all give the quality of strong rhythmic design that one finds in the landscapes of Cézanne.

NICOLAS POUSSIN. ORPHEUS AND EURYDICE. (*Fig. 23; Rm. XIV, No. 740.*)

Landscape painting received a great impetus in the seventeenth century, through the work of Poussin, Claude Lorrain, Rubens and the Dutch. The human figure lost the all-absorbing interest it had held during the humanistic Renaissance, and nature, which had usually been given a subordinate position in the background, now came definitely to the fore. (Patinir, Brueghel and a few others had emphasized landscape before, but the tendency had not be-

FIG. 22. ST. JEROME
By Lotto

come general.) For a long time the human figures remained as necessary parts of a landscape — nature was not quite interesting enough without them — but they were reduced to smaller, more incidental parts. They were still (in Poussin and Claude) classical in form and in the stories they represented; but the story, and the title of the picture, are of little consequence. Poussin's human figures, even when small, are more interesting in themselves than Claude's, because more actively, gracefully drawn. They reflect Raphael's influence in these qualities, but their attitudes are original, varied and graphic. (Notice the girl recoiling from the snake, the fisherman, and the distant boatmen and bathers.) As contrasted with Rubens, both Poussin and Claude preserved on the whole the calm serenity of Giorgione and Titian in their landscapes. But Poussin's color is less warmly glowing than Claude's: it is nearer to Veronese than to Titian in its use of bright clear blues and cooler greens. Occasionally, superficial color detaches his figures from their backgrounds, but here a gentle, pale gold light tones down and unifies the colors with comparative success.

One of Poussin's best traits, quite evident in this picture, is the clear, definite structure he gives to a landscape, by dividing it into contrasting planes of light and dark. He defines the contours of each individual figure, house or tree more sharply than Claude, who tends to melt them a little more into one general atmosphere. This sharpness does not go so far as to be edgy or linear; it is much less detailed than in Patinir. Each object is solidly built up of light and color as well as line; but it is realized as a definite unit in itself. Alternately light and dark, with a few softening gradations between, the planes recede into distance step by step, and fit together into subordinate groups of figures, trees and houses. Even individual leaves are sometimes

FIG. 23. ORPHEUS AND EURYDICE

By Poussin

brought out, as here on the right. But plain expanses elsewhere restore a general sense of largeness. Concealed repetitions of shape among people and hills, trees and clouds knit the picture firmly together as design. As in Claude, the effect is of a neatly trimmed, parklike expanse, not of wild nature.

CLAUDE LORRAIN. CLEOPATRA DISEMBARKING AT TARSUS. (*Fig. 24; Rm. XIV, No. 314.*)

Claude's distinctive qualities, mentioned in comparing him with Poussin, are all embodied in this picture. The figures are unusually animated for a Claude, but bear less relation to the contours of the landscape than in the Poussin. He considered them of so little importance that he often left them to be inserted by some assistant. All through the picture, there is less detachment of individual parts, less rhythmic recurrence of similar contours, more reliance on a soft, pervasive glow of sunlight to unify the picture. This is especially true as we approach the source of the light, which is not visible in the Poussin. Nearby the forms are silhouetted, but as they recede their outlines melt together in the sunset haze. There is more depth, more spacious grandeur, and less clear-cut compactness. But the softening effects of atmosphere are not carried to anything like the extreme of Turner or Monet.

The design is still basically one of definite lines and planes, over which the sunset plays. It brings out the forms of architecture with distinct shadows, and those of the boats and persons with delicate outlines of gold. As in Carpaccio's harbor-view, which it strongly resembles, the scene is knit together by long diagonals — the slanting yard-arms on the left, and on the right converging perspective lines. It is further knit by tall vertical masts and walls, and by the

FIG. 24. CLEOPATRA DISEMBARKING AT TARSUS
By Claude Lorrain

short curves of ship-hulls, trees and human figures. There is less pageantry of costumes than in Carpaccio, but his basic form survives in the expanse of quiet water bordered by towering classical buildings, and peopled with leisurely, dignified groups in classical attire. It survives, too, in the skill with which space is punctuated, marked off at rhythmic intervals by series of similar objects, so that every region between here and the horizon is felt as a different part of space. The lack of such marking off makes the view from a ship at sea, with nothing but water in all directions, seem comparatively small and monotonous. Here a series of boats leads us step by step to the sunset on the left, while on the right we are similarly led by the row of houses and the scattered groups of people. A relatively small area, thus organized, can be made to seem vast, unified and interesting. The practical arts of formal gardening and landscape architecture, at Versailles, for example, owe much to the principles of space composition worked out by landscape painters.

WATTEAU. THE EMBARKATION FOR CYTHERA. (*Fig. 25; Rm. XVI, No. 982.*)

Like those of his followers, Lancret, Boucher and Fragonard, Watteau's typical paintings are light, delicate and artificial. They express the same spirit and subject-matter: dainty silk-clad aristocrats, pretty shepherds and shepherdesses, and a perpetual round of gay, thoughtless amusement. In form, they run to elaborate ornamentation with short, broken swirls, and color that is pale, soft and thin. These general traits are apparent in the picture shown. But Watteau is nearer than his followers to the Venetians, with warm red-browns, dark green and gold instead of pink, white and pale blue, and with soft, melting atmosphere

FIG. 25. THE EMBARKATION FOR CYTHERA

By Watteau

instead of porcelain-like, sculptural fragility. More than the rest, too, he continues the landscape tradition of Claude Lorrain, with its deep, park-like vistas and its towering, gracefully bending trees. But the classical majesty is gone, and the firmness of structure, both dissolved in a lilting flutter of ribbons, leaves and Cupids' wings. The painting is appropriately thin and sketchy, with almost the transparency of water-color, especially in the background, where a wash of dull brown and green serves to heighten the soft glistening folds of pale red and blue silk. To follow the line of little figures from right to left, and to read in their dainty gesturings a progressive story of romantic courtship, is like listening to Weber's *Invitation to the Dance*, or to some minuet of Rameau, wistful, sprightly and ephemeral. The color, light and texture of things are in perfect harmony with this theme: never very solid, but comparatively so on the right, where the lovers are still urging and hesitating, with coy starts and backward looks; then ever more ethereal as the procession moves on to the boat and the hovering Cupids, until all shapes are lost in pale blue and gold clouds above the lake, and in mountain peaks hardly less vaporous.

FRANCOIS BOUCHER. DIANA BATHING. (*Fig. 26; Rm. XVI, No. 30.*)

The majority of Bouchers are mere wall-ornaments, stereotyped variations of a formula for artificial prettiness. They represent a late stage in the thinning-out of Renaissance classicism. Greek goddesses are transformed into dolls that simper in weak, empty affectation. The warm rich bodies that Titian and Rubens gave them have faded to a plastery pink and white, and the vigorous action of Poussin has dwindled to a flutter of wavy ribbons. All

FIG. 26. DIANA BATHING

By Boucher

textures acquire the same hard shallowness: roses are tinselly, rocks and trees like a photographer's back-drop. There is always a clearly organized linear pattern, accurately balanced, but it is imitative and overloaded with small ornaments.

The *Diana* is one of his few pictures that rise above this level, not to lofty heights, but to a fairly well-developed and original form. Preserving the dainty lightness characteristic of his school, and his own lively rhythm of small swirls and diagonals, it backs them up with deeper color, especially in the realistic pile of game and the large blue cloth. The human flesh-tints are not plastery, but a fine porcelain, suffused with peach and rose, and the landscape harmonizes in a soft, cloudy gray-green. Above all, the picture is not over-ornamented, and the graceful design of masses stands out with relative strength and simplicity.

CHARDIN. STILL LIFE: VARIOUS UTENSILS. (*Fig. 27; Rm. XVI, No. 101.*)

A genuine taste for still-life painting is one of the surest signs of a direct appreciation of pictorial form. There the external, secondary appeal of story and human associations is slight, and the principal appeal, if any, must be made through the more intrinsic qualities of the design itself. Especially in the case of Chardin, there is comparatively little tendency to choose objects interesting for their associations, such as quaint old musical instruments, dead game and the like (the inferior *Monkey Antiquary*, 97, is an exception). Commonplace utensils, fruit and plain dishes serve his purpose quite as well. Nor does he rely on the other, somewhat specious appeal of literal, microscopically exact representation: tiny drops of dew on a leaf, or tiny cracks in a bowl, to win applause for his virtuosity. He paints, on the whole,

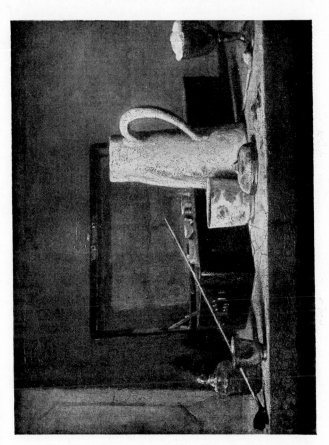

FIG. 27. STILL LIFE
By Chardin

rather broadly, leaving out small surface details and trying to bring out, rather, the distinctive, deep-lying qualities of each substance, and its relation to the whole design. In a general way, he relies somewhat on our past experience: if we had not seen and handled many peaches, we could not appreciate how well he expresses the essential qualities of a peach in *Basket of Peaches* (102). More vividly than in any actual peach, we are made to notice here the dull gray, furry bloom on its surface, the blended reds and yellows of the skin, the firm, soft roundness underneath. The bowl and pitcher in *Various Utensils* are far from photographic, yet their distinctive texture is somehow realized and contrasted with those of the box and pipe. In this deeply realistic painting of textures, as well as in his *genre* scenes of homelike intimacy (e.g., *Grace*, 92), Chardin is the heir of the 17th century Dutch, especially Vermeer, de Hooch and Terborch. His reliance on plain, simple strength, without ostentatious ornament, expresses the spirit of a sturdy middle-class, in marked contrast with that of the other 18th century French painters.

The appeal of such a picture as *Various Utensils* is not only realistic but decorative. A small, detached fragment of it would be treasured for its rich tints even though its representative meaning were unknown. Greatest of all is its appeal as an organized design. Each object is distinctly set in its own small bit of space, at its own relative distance from the eye. Linear themes are repeated and contrasted: the straight lines of the box, pipe-stems, pitcher and bowl; the short curves of the pitcher-handle, pipe-bowls, glass and silver cup. The flat rectangles of the box and shelf are opposed to the rounded planes of the dishes. In color, the themes are the dull blue of the box-lining and the streaks of pitcher and bowl, the reddish and grayish browns of glass, bottle and shelf. So strongly built is the architecture of the group that not a detail could be altered, one feels, without spoiling it. Emphasis and subordination (often missing in a poor still-life) are preserved throughout: some few parts, here the pitcher and bowl, are always raised by light and color to a climax, while others are plainer, darker, duller in various degrees.

INGRES. ODALISQUE. (*Fig. 28; Rm. VIII, No. 422b.*)

The French revolution swept away, for a time at least, the gay frivolities of the old régime. It also brought new fashions and new ideals in art. In particular, it brought a desire to be like the ancient Romans, in military power, in austerity of manners, in dress and in furniture. Ingres and David (*Mme. Récamier, No. 199*) are the painters of this neo-classical revival. Their art is unlike that of ancient Rome at its best; for its coloring is hard, superficial and monotonous. Its distinctive traits of form, as contrasted with eighteenth century court painting, are comparative plainness of surface, and long, sweeping lines. These imply the omission of elaborate ornament and of all the flowery little broken swirls and curlicues dear to Boucher and Fragonard.

This painting by Ingres is, in subject, no more austere than a Boucher; but its treatment is austere. Its coloring and texture are cold, metallic. There is no Venetian warmth to the flesh, and it rests against draperies of steely blue, pale gold and white, stiffly folded and devoid of mellowing tints. The body is like marble, with a slight coating of pink; but it lacks even the sensuous charm of late Greek sculpture, which is sensitively modelled with slight undulations of surface, producing soft shadows. Here the modelling is plain and hard, with no delicate gradations between light and dark. The face is a regular, impersonal, expressionless

FIG. 28. ODALISQUE

By Ingres

mask, and the body is also too smoothly regular in its lines to be realistic or individual.

Lacking all these modes of appeal, which are possessed by other pictures of similar subject, it is forced to rely largely on the intrinsic beauty of its lines as lines. Considered in themselves, they do make a pattern of unusual grace. To follow in imagination the artist's hand as he drew these long, sinuous, intertwining curves is to feel one's hand going through the gestures of a stately dance. It is to feel a distinctive linear music, of a kind less intricate than the Gothic, less vivacious and fanciful than Botticelli's, less rugged than Dürer's, a little cold and formal, like the rest of the picture — a suavely dignified melody that is peculiar to Ingres.

DELACROIX. ALGERIAN WOMEN. (*Fig. 29; Rm. VIII, No. 210.*)

Delacroix is known as the painter of Romanticism, and Ingres as that of Classicism. While these terms are too ambiguous to be of much use in criticism, they have certain definite meanings in regard to these two men. The essential difference here is not one of subject-matter: this picture and the *Odalisque* by Ingres are both of languid, voluptuous women of the harem; so are *The Turkish Bath,* by Ingres, and *The Death of Sardanapalus,* by Delacroix. But Ingres treats the subject with an emphasis on sharp firm line and static, sculptural modelling; Delacroix with an emphasis on rich melting color and strenuous movement. Ingres is the heir of Raphael, the Florentines and David; Delacroix of the Venetians and Rubens. The picture shown is untypical in its lack of dramatic action; but it is typical and important for its color. Even in black and white, one can see the easy relaxation, the living postures of the women,

FIG. 29. ALGERIAN WOMEN
By Delacroix

and the use of soft shadows instead of sharp lines. In the
original, one feels in certain spots the vibrant, sparkling
effect of color and light, due largely to the close juxtaposition of many rough, coarse brush-strokes of contrasting colors. The cushion in the lower left-hand corner is especially
notable for this quality, and for the reflected sunlight on
its bright-colored surface. There is a fine silky, shimmering surface quality in all the textiles, both gauzy veils and
heavy brocades. His technique of broken color Delacroix
owed largely to Constable, and later on it was further
developed by the impressionists.

CLAUDE MONET. THE REGATTA AT ARGENTEUIL.
(*Fig. 30; Camondo Collection, No. 180.*)

The best works of Monet, from a standpoint of strong design, are not always his most original or typical, or the ones
by which his greatest influence has been exerted. His most
original contribution is the rendering of the effects of sunlight on the surfaces of colored objects out of doors. In addition, he develops a technique suited to that purpose: large
strokes of contrasting color side by side, or superimposed
but not quite mixed, so that the eye at a distance feels them
as a pervasive, iridescent vibration. These two things he did
so well and so originally in the early seventies as to bring
about a revolution in the art of painting. But as a rule, he
was content to specialize on them alone, and to neglect
three-dimensional design, either dissolving all shapes in a
luminous mist of color, or choosing some ready-made, simple
pattern on which to embroider his surface qualities. Occasionally he works out an original deep-space design of some
force: in the *Gare St. Lazare* (*Salle Caillebotte*) the slop-
ing roof of the railway station, the tracks and distant
puffs of steam, build up a firm though delicate arrangement

FIG. 30. THE REGATTA AT ARGENTEUIL

By Monet

in space. But such achievements did not seem to interest him, and through most of his life, until the end, he was content to specialize on surface-reflections, either embroidering them on some ready-made, simple pattern in the scene at hand, or dissolving all shapes in a luminous mist of color. In the views of the *Cathedral of Rouen*, here and in the *Salle Caillebotte*, the element of design is contributed by the architectural façade itself, on whose surface Monet spread the sun-tints of various hours of the day. In a series of *Water-lilies* (Camondo) he also takes a ready-made pattern of a bridge over water, and varies it only in surface-color.

A picture like *The Regatta at Argenteuil* is thoroughly typical of his dominant interest, although less rich in texture than some of his later works. It shows clearly, even in black and white, the emphasis on sunlight reflections, the large, sketchy brush-strokes, the vagueness of objects, chiefly at the right, and the lack of organized design. The use of the broken color technique is chiefly at the right, in the houses, trees and shore and their reflections. The more than natural intensity of color everywhere, especially in the red houses, and the use of colored shadows, mostly violet and blue, are other qualities characteristic of Monet and the impressionists generally.

RENOIR. AT THE MOULIN DE LA GALETTE. (*Fig. 31; Salle Caillebotte.*)

In this vibrant study of sunlight falling through leaves on a crowd of dancers, the impressionist movement reached one of its highest peaks. Later on (as in *The Nymphs*, in this room) Renoir developed an interest in solid modelling, non-realistic color and distortion which took him out of the class of pure impressionists. Here the interest in sunlight reflections still dominates, although it is enriched by a wealth of varied content, expressive and decorative, such as no other of the impressionists could achieve. The impressionist aim of representing outdoor light on colored objects is achieved with amazing brilliance. The flecks of summer sunshine, falling through young green leaves, with here and there a larger splash of dazzling, clear light, have more of the actual radiance of spring than had ever been captured in paint before.

But the picture is far more than an imitation, or even an intensified expression of natural sunlight. Its harmony of colors, especially of blue, is an independent pictorial creation. All the blues of past art — those which fill the clear spaces of Piero della Francesca; those which Veronese and Velazquez use to cool the warmth of Titian's reds; and those which Vermeer takes over in pure cobalt intensity from Chinese porcelain — all these and others are here, transformed by a new soft lightness. They stand out in vivid intensity against a pale rose dress or a bright yellow hat, or blend with these hues in countless iridescent tints and filmy, Goya-like textures — faint lavender shadows and reflections on silk; a blue-green dress that changes in color like a black opal; violet and opal shadows in blond hair, and pale yellow-green spring foliage. All these rainbow colors are set in motion by the dancing flecks of sunlight, and by the lightly poised gestures of the young dancers.

Renoir was never more human, never less the specialist in abstract forms or more the young Parisian artist, than in this representation of a scene he knew and enjoyed, with frank interest in its subject-matter. In few of his other pictures are the figures so active; here all is lively merriment, dance and light conversation — the spirit of Watteau, with realism added to gaiety. Every figure is deftly set down in some distinctive attitude and facial expression, with a few

FIG. 31. AT THE MOULIN DE LA GALETTE

By Renoir

casual touches. A hundred details are thus brought into reality, expressing the spirit of the scene as well as forming beautiful color-chords — the green glasses with orange drinks; the little girl with fine gold hair; the blasé squint of the young man dancing at the left; everywhere smiles, coquetries and attentive listening. Each is made to live in itself and is blended into the concentrated essence of many remembered scenes from life.

As in some of Goya's bull-fight scenes, the effect of a large and bustling crowd is conveyed with relatively few individualized figures. The contrast between these and the vague streaks and smudges which indicate the rest is bridged over by forms intermediate in distinctness. These graded accents, along with skilled alternation of colors, lights and shadows, help to organize the scene in space with all appropriate clarity, in spite of the sketchiness and flickering sunshine. There is no definite pattern of lines or masses. This makes for a certain diffuse fluidity; but the picture is unified by other factors: definite themes of color and light, and its own ethereal, quivering rhythm of motion.

DEGAS. THE STAR. (*Fig. 32; Camondo Collection, No. 217.*)

While most of the impressionists were melting away all definite outlines in their luminous mists, Degas was carrying on the Goya-Daumier tradition of terse linear illustration. He loved to draw race-horses and ballet-dancers, and in a few irregular, sketchy strokes to express the light, tense agility of both. His early works are comparatively realistic, and in oil; they emphasize delicacy and grace. The later ones are mostly in pastel, and represent his models in bizarre, strained postures, full of unusual, striking repetitions of angle and curve. There is brutal naturalism in their lack of physi-

FIG. 32. THE STAR
By Degas

cal beauty; but the coloring in these late pastels — rich blends of intense hues in a dry, chalky fresco-like surface — is decorative in the extreme. Of the early group, an outstanding example is No. 160, *The Opera Dancing School;* of the later, *Woman Drying her Neck* (226).

The Star represents a transitional period between the two. It has the grace and fluffy delicacy of texture of the early works, with more breadth and simplification. Its composition is deliberately one-sided, unbalanced, but linked together by repeated angles (e.g., the ballet-skirt and the large umbrellas). The color shows greater intensity, with concentrated blotches of bright color in the flowers. Realistic theatre-lighting still floods the star's face and arms; but elsewhere it is giving way to a more decorative interest in pure color-contrasts.

Briefer Mention

Italian (in Salles IV, VII and VI): TITIAN, *The Entombment* (1584); *The Supper at Emmaus* (1581), works of the highest rank, combining rich, deep, organic color and glowing atmosphere, complex, monumentally balanced arrangement of figures, and a restrained, majestic drama of human emotions. TINTORETTO, *Susannah* (1464); *Paradise* (1465) — the former is typical in its bizarrely unsymmetrical, oblique composition; the latter an intricate design of many figures, organized by continuous, agitated movements of line, and by contrasts of delicate, rich color into subordinate groups, all fitting together as parts of a Dantesque vision of epic grandeur. VERONESE, *The Wedding-feast at Cana* (1192) a huge crowd skillfully organized in space, full of brilliant, variegated costumes, and expressing an air of elegant luxury. SIMONE MARTINI, *The Ascent to Calvary* (1383) and FRA

ANGELICO, *Martyrdom of Sts. Cosmo and Damien* (1293) — decorative patterns of bright, flat, contrasting colors. PISANELLO, *Princess of the Este Family* (1422a) — a finely engraved, cameo-like profile, against a gaily fanciful flat background of bright-colored flowers and butterflies. COSIMO TURA, *Pietà* (1556) — intense Gothic pathos in bold, incisive, rhythmic lines. PERUGINO, *Combat of Love and Chastity* (1567) — feathery trees and languidly graceful figures, clearly arranged in deep space. ALBERTINELLI, *Christ and Magdalen* (1115) — delicate, gentle tenderness, in graceful, floating gestures and a soft, silver-blue landscape dotted with lacy trees. CARPACCIO, *St. Stephen Preaching* (1211) — strong, rhythmic space composition, unifying a broad vista of figures, hills and architecture. BOTTICELLI, *Giovanna Albizzi and the Three Graces* (1297) — decorative linear arabesque and dry, light fresco tints.

Spanish, Flemish, Dutch and *German* (Salles VI, VII, VIII, XIX–XXXV): EL GRECO, *Christ on the Cross and Donor* (1729) — color drab, but a hint of his intense, agitated force in streaks of lurid light and in writhing bodily distortions. VELAZQUEZ, *The Infanta Margherita* (1731) — a hint of his power to create delicate substances, in a few broad strokes of rose and gray. RUBENS, *The Kermesse* (2115) — this and the small pictures near it, rather than the grandiose *Marie de Medici* series, show Rubens at his best; a vigorous, lilting swirl of muscular, lusty bodies against a rolling landscape; richly colored and vital, but not bombastic. VAN EYCK, *Virgin and Donor* (1986) — exquisite miniature perfection in faces and landscape, along with strength and simplicity resulting from substantial color-texture and clear selective emphasis on most important parts. FRANS HALS, *The Bohemian Girl* (2384) — a vivacious, colorful portrait, in quick, simplified, dashing strokes. REMBRANDT, *Hendrickje Stoffels* (2547) and *The Supper at Emmaus* (2539) — sombre colors, blended subtly with golden light, produce a portrait of rich surface texture, and a simple drama enacted in mysterious, glowing twilight. VERMEER, *The Lacemaker* (2456) — a design of delicate, contrasting color-textures, light, pale and cool, but deeply substantial; lines and planes fit together in a converging pattern. DÜRER, *Self-portrait* (Salle XXXIII) — nervous vitality in its wavering outlines, and rugged strength in its irregular modelling with scattered shadows. HOLBEIN, *Anne of Cleves* (2718) — a brilliant surface pattern of heavily ornamented color-strips, arranged in repeated sweeping, converging curves.

French (Salles X–XVI, VIII, I–III, XXXVII–XXXIX, Camondo, Caillebotte): SCHOOL OF AVIGNON, *Pietà* (1001B) — a striking design of long, rigid limbs, boldly carved in sculptural planes and built into an ellipse full of swaying angles. FOUQUET, *Charles VII* (289) — again a sculptural design, of deeply grooved cloth-folds in fan-like radiation, with a gorgeous color-pattern of dark contrasting wine-red, blue, green, black and gold; a massively carved, expressive head above it. FRANÇOIS CLOUET, *Charles IX* (128) — more delicately worked, in light, floating lines and softly tinted, lustrous textures. FROMENT, *The Resurrection of Lazarus* (Salle X) — a monumental arrangement of figures in relation to hills and castle-towers; Flemish in basis, but with delicate French coloring. LOUIS LE NAIN, *Family of Peasants* (Salle XII) — plain, solid, vigorous naturalism, brusquely rejecting suave classical grace and formal pattern; yet firmly rhythmic in its angular masses, and enriched by solid color that brings out hidden lustre in homely materials. FRAGONARD, *The Music Lesson* (291); *Bathers* (293) — more substantial than most of their school; the former a simple design of long diagonals in soft pastel reds; the latter a light, dainty version of the Rubens-Boucher swirl, in melting green and rose. LANCRET, *The Music Lesson* (468) — in delicate, pale pastel tints and long firm lines; slight but harmonious and distinctive. DAUMIER, *Scapin and Crispin* (122) — bizarre and fantastic, in long curving streaks of blended shadow and dull, iridescent color; tersely expressive in face and gesture. COROT, *Dancing Nymphs* (138, Salle VIII); *The Belfry of Douai* and *The Coliseum* (141, 140 in Salle XXXVII) — The first is the familiar, romantic Corot, a delicate, lyrical version of Claude Lorrain, with gracefully swaying, fluffy, gray-green trees, silvery mists, and nymphs in pale rose-and-blue gowns. The others are the stronger Corot, of well-defined, rhythmic masses, clear lights and distinct space-intervals. COURBET, *Roe-deer in a Wood* (145); *The Painter's Studio* (143) — classic and romantic artificialities abandoned, and nature seen afresh; one is a landscape with realistic animals blended into its rich, clear, mossy-green and silver-gray depths; the other a monumental figure-composition, with unidealized men and women, varied and expressive in pose, built into a design with apparent casualness. MANET, *Olympia* (613); *Portrait of Zola* (both in Salle Caillebotte) — luminous, flattened planes of color, rhythmic in outline, contrasted in light and dark, combining realism with decoration, Spanish and Japanese with impressionist influences. CÉZANNE, *L'Estaque* (Caillebotte); *Apples and Oranges* (Camondo) — Impressionist brilliance of light and color, built into organic designs of solid masses in deep space, firmly knit by concealed rhythmic repetitions of theme.

Oriental: PERSIAN, INDIAN AND ARABIAN miniatures and book illuminations, in the *Salle Musulman.* CHINESE AND JAPANESE paintings and prints in the *Musée*

d'extrême Orient. In the latter, works of HOKUSAI, HIRO-
SHIGE, and anonymous painters of the Sung and Ming
dynasties in China.

The Luxembourg Museum

Devoted to recent art, and a testing-ground for doubtful
reputations in painting, this museum periodically shifts its
contents — the accepted few to the Louvre, and the rest to
obscurity. It gives a fair sampling of all the chief present-
day styles and tendencies, conservative and radical. The best
examples of the impressionist movement, radical in the
seventies and eighties, have recently been transferred to the
Salle Caillebotte in the Louvre. There remain four main
distinguishable groups. One is the conservative, academic
tradition of exact representation and story-telling interest.
It fills the first few rooms near the entrance. Farther on
are the remaining impressionist works: chief of which are
L'Église de Vetheuil, by MONET; *Les bords du Loing,* by
SISLEY; and *Liseuse,* by RENOIR. Then come the neo-
impressionists and early post-impressionists. The former are
represented by SEURAT, with *The Circus,* and by SIGNAC,
with *Le château des papes;* both in large, distinct, regular,
contrasting spots of color that sparkle vividly. Among the
latter are TOULOUSE-LAUTREC, with *Jeune femme ac-
croupie,* bizarre in linear pattern but delicate in shimmering pastel tints; GAUGUIN, with *Le cheval blanc,* a decorative screen in blunt primitive drawing and flat, exotically
clashing color-areas. In Room 8 and neighboring rooms
are shown the contemporary radicals who have achieved a
certain degree of established reputation. Beside the one discussed below, there are examples by UTRILLO (*Vue
d'Anse*), BRACQUE, DE SEGONZAC, ROUAULT, VLAMINCK
and DERAIN.

HENRI MATISSE. ODALISQUE. (*Fig. 33.*)

Essentially based on color, a picture by Matisse must be seen in the original to be appreciated. In black and white, one is at first conscious of little more than the extreme distortions and simplifications: the picture seems only a childish daub. Even in color, it will seem crude and shocking to persons used only to the darker, softer tints of conventional painting. Here the effect is violent, barbaric, loud, clashing, like the dress of gypsies and South Sea Islanders. But to persons whose habits are not fixed, these clashes usually come in time to seem refreshing, stimulating and even harmonious in their own way, like the discords of modern music. One of the best ways to approach them is through a study of primitive textiles, the South Sea paintings of Gauguin, and, more especially, Persian miniatures. All these are sources of Matisse's art, in addition to the impressionists, whose bright, sunny colors and distortions of shape, now accepted, were once thought shockingly ugly. There is little or no richness or realism of texture in Matisse's individual areas of color; but taken all together, they form a brilliant pattern of contrasts, comparable to the Persian, but full of original and surprising transitions. Like a Persian miniature, also, the picture is divided into definite sections contrasting in texture: the floor a uniform flat red; the couch striped green and brown; the walls brightly decorated in all-over patterns of blue on white, red on yellow; the garments are of red with yellow flowers, and pale green with yellow flowers. Only a few parts are solidly modelled, and these with shadows bizarrely unrealistic; but the picture is not flat, for the planes of wall, couch and figure are carefully arranged in space at different angles. Linear themes further knit the composition together as design: for example, the pointed curves of which the figure is made, against the rectangles of the couch and

FIG. 33. ODALISQUE
By Matisse

background. The outstanding differences from Persian art are traceable to impressionism: a broad, rough, sketchy stroke, and an occasional trace of sunshine. The latter, however, is used not for its intrinsic appeal, but as one of many different ways of varying the parts of a design in color and texture.

Other Pictures in Paris

Musée des Arts Decoratifs: usually open on days when other museums are closed; contains the famous *Déjeuner sur l'herbe,* by MANET, and other impressionist, Barbizon and romantic paintings of secondary importance; Japanese prints, medieval stained glass and tapestry. The *Bibliothèque Nationale* contains medieval and Renaissance manuscript illuminations of great value, and many modern engravings. Selected examples of all these are exhibited under glass. The *Musée Guimet* is devoted mainly to oriental sculpture, but contains some Chinese paintings on the second floor. The *Musée de Cluny* is devoted to sculpture and applied arts of the middle ages and Renaissance; but its tapestries, glassware, porcelains, wood-carvings and metal-work afford excellent opportunities to study the adaptation of pictorial forms to various materials and media. The *Louvre* also contains fine examples of these arts. A special interest in medieval stained glass can be followed up in the *Sainte Chapelle;* but the world's finest glass can be seen only by travelling to the cathedral at Chartres. Among the works of individual painters scattered through Paris, one should see at the *Panthéon* the murals of PUVIS DE CHAVANNES, on the life of St. Genevieve; and in the *Church of St. Sulpice* those of DELACROIX, *Jacob Wrestling with the Angel* and *Heliodorus Expelled from the Temple.*

OUTSIDE PARIS

A catalogue of art in the smaller French towns would be endless; each of the chief provincial cities contains its own museum, emphasizing works produced in that region. At *Dijon*, for example, the collection of miscellaneous paintings is inferior, but that of ancient Burgundian art is unique and excellent.

One of the most interesting provincial museums is the *Condé*, at *Chantilly*. This contains the delightful *Book of Hours of the Duke of Berry*, with its miniatures on the months of the year, by POL DE LIMBOURG, a fifteenth century Fleming. They are strong and original in design, delicate in tint, and full of fresh, realistic landscape feeling. In addition, it contains important miniatures by FOUQUET and other French primitives.

One who wishes to see the oldest paintings in existence can travel to the *Dordogne* in southern France, and study the PREHISTORIC CAVE DRAWINGS in the Caverns of Combarelles and Fond de Gaume, then over into Spain to see those at Altamira. If he has not seen reproductions, he will be surprised at their terse rendering of the essentials of animal structure and movement, at their fluently rhythmic brush-strokes and delicate polychrome shading.

CHAPTER III

SPAIN

MADRID

If one goes to Spain to see pictures at all, it is to see El
Greco, Velazquez and Goya. Madrid has other treasures,
but one can find their like elsewhere. These three men, all
of high standing in the history of their art, are at their
best only in Spain. That best is here in such variety and
profusion as to spread three great careers before us at
once; there is no need to piece them out, as in studying
other painters, from one's memories of a dozen different
cities. The effect is so engrossing as to hold one's attention
within narrow limits, and to make one pass by, almost
unseeing, luxurious Venetians and others of the highest
quality.

By train from Paris, one passes rapidly through a country
north of Madrid, dotted with small towns rich in tradition
and architecture, such as Burgos, Segovia and Avila. Each
has its own little altar-paintings or small collection of Spanish
primitives, worth seeing on a leisurely trip. Southward, in
Seville, and eastward, in Barcelona, there are good provincial
museums. In the former Murillo is shown to better advantage than in his popular, sentimental pictures, and in the

latter (a good stopping-off place on the way to Italy) a group of Catalonian and other primitives offers a more specialized interest. On the whole, however, the best pictures are so well concentrated in and about Madrid that little travel is necessary. To study El Greco thoroughly, one must make two short trips out of town, to Toledo and the Escorial. But the Prado contains many typical Grecos, and all the chief works of Velazquez and Goya.

The Prado Museum

For sheer splendor of coloring, direct and immediate in its effect upon the senses, there is no room in the world to compare with the main Velazquez room in the Prado. Every color of the rainbow and the sunset is there, as fresh and unfaded as if the paint were scarcely dry. But unlike the sunset, their charm endures and increases with longer looking. They are not merely bright and intense, but organized into complex designs which heighten the intrinsic power of each color, and add the further delight of subtle transitions and harmonies. Still more, they appeal through association, by reminding us of every rich texture we have seen and touched, and by creating a roomful of human beings that seem to be more alive and individual than any ordinary flesh-and-blood assemblage. The versatility of these paintings is amazing; they seem to include every possible style and technique, from the early Renaissance to modern impressionism, and each with a light, inimitable ease of touch.

One must visit the Grecos and Goyas in neighboring rooms to discover two qualities lacking in Velazquez: dynamic energy of movement, and intensity of emotional expression. Velazquez is quiet, aloof, impersonal; these others are narrower but more human in their aspirations and

FIG. 34. THE SPINNERS

By Velazquez

passions. In addition, they speak, as he does, the direct
language of visible form.

VELAZQUEZ. THE SPINNERS. (*Fig. 34; No. 1173.*)

This and *The Maids of Honor* are the crowning achievements of Velazquez's last and greatest years. Specialized
effects to which he had devoted whole pictures, often neglecting to develop them into fully balanced designs, are here
combined in monumental complexity. The spirit of Titian
fills the *Spinners* with a soft haze of dull reds, russets and
golden browns, and gives to its plain peasant-women a spontaneous, unaffected classical grace of gesture; so that, even
more than the gentlewomen standing in the doorway, they
are of one race with the Renaissance goddesses on the distant
tapestry. No one has shown more clearly than Velazquez,
that honest naturalism in art need not imply a taste for
physical ugliness.

The bit of tapestry in the lighted alcove sets the theme for
the whole composition. Its diagonal curves are developed,
with more sweeping breadth and power, in the converging
diagonal rhythms of the foreground. Its concentrated, ornate
richness of color, its gleams of daylight on silvery gray-blue,
dull rose and olive, are gently diffused over the standing
ladies (almost indistinguishable from the tapestry) to the
spacious plainness of the dimly lit work-room. Here there is
another masterly system of graded accents, from the gray-
green wall with its hanging skeins of yarn and its ladder
(scarcely raised above it in tone) through the shadowy, flat,
red-skirted woman in the center, to the girl winding yarn
at the right. This girl, with strongly lighted and rounded
waist, with skirt of green intenser than the walls, her body
swaying in the natural dance-rhythm of her work, is the
climax of the composition.

VELAZQUEZ. THE MAIDS OF HONOR. (*Fig. 35; No. 1174.*)

This is so distinctly in the world of Vermeer and de Hooch that one is tempted to infer Dutch influence. But these men were at the start of their careers when Velazquez painted it, near the end of his; and the great Dutchmen of the time — Hals and Rembrandt — worked in quite different veins. This is the form on which the seventeenth century Dutch *genre* painters later specialized: a homelike, realistic family group, drawn in short, irregular curves without classical grace, against a plain interior full of rectangular planes at different angles; cool, clear daylight from a side-window to bring out richly colored textiles against plain, dull, gray-green walls.

For the source of the design and its cool, juicy green coloring we must look back as far as Jan Van Eyck. But here is no miniature painting: even a Vermeer seems detailed and literal by comparison with its swift, sketchy, flattening abbreviations. The distinctive qualities of textures are brought out, not by meticulous copying, thread by thread and hair by hair, but by the most terse and simplified presenting of essentials. Looked at closely, the Princess's hair is but a blur of yellow paint; the hoop-skirts are gray-green smears. But at a little distance they become, as if by magic, the fine gold hair of a child, brushed flat and dropping in a fluffy cloud, and the stiff folds of heavy, dull-finished silk. It is not only surfaces that are rendered: the whole object, rarefied or dense, is given three-dimensional reality at its proper point in space by blended color and light.

As to composition: the Dutch *genre* painters rarely attempted designs so spacious and complex. The row of children forms a large triangle of brightly lighted areas, whose apex is the distant doorway. On each side nearby, the scene

FIG. 35. THE MAIDS OF HONOR
By Velazquez

is framed with a tall upright area of light. In the middle distance, other forms are disposed with skillfully graded intermediate accents: the ecclesiastical pair, vaguely sketched in flat shadows; the dimly glistening mirror that reflects the King and Queen watching from where the observer stands; Velazquez himself, painting. A splash of bright red paint on his palette, and other spots of red in bits of embroidery and ribbon, stand out against the green, and help to link the scattered figures with a loose but rhythmic bond of color.

El Greco. The Pentecost. (*Frontispiece; No. 828.*)

Color is the basic factor in this picture. It is at the opposite extreme from such pictures as Holbein's *Jane Seymour*, where the design is first drawn in sharp outlines, and color then laid between them, as a hard, superficial addition. Here there are no continuously sharp outlines: the picture is built up of broad streaks of color, more or less indefinite and melting at the edges. One's attention is drawn, not to these edges, but to the narrow streaks of lighter, brighter color which emerge from the darker, broader ones, again with soft melting edges, to represent long highlights on limbs and garment-folds. These long streaks act as lines, in giving shape and direction to the movements. Tintoretto had used streaks of light in such a way, but here they are less like natural reflections on flesh and cloth; the Venetian interest in realistic textures is gone. These garments are not cloth, but sheets of vaporous flame, wrapping bodies hardly more solid. The heads and arms themselves are translucent, phosphorescent, as if composed of luminous gases in some intricate pyrotechnic display. They reflect no natural light, but seem to glow from within. The shadows themselves are luminous, glowing more sombrely in deep blue-greens and crimsons. Sometimes they are in hues contrasting with those of the highlights, to form an iridescent shimmer of greenish gold and violet. Color thus makes a direct appeal in itself, rather than as an imitation of some well-known material.

Yet it is not mere abstract decoration. It ceases to be paint, and creates the illusion of some strange ghostly substance out there in space. It is just realistic enough to convey the essentials of its Biblical story, with all the emotional associations attached. It is a bridge between the world seen and the supernatural world imagined, and thus expresses the visions of a religious mystic in a fervidly religious age.

Expressing the same spirit, the rhythms of movement not only form a decorative pattern, but convey a mood of agitated aspiration. The basic arrangement of figures is fairly symmetrical and stable, with a horizontal row of heads that further tends to restrain movement. The design is one of intersecting triangles. The two men below, and the central one above, stand out as a triangular pattern in themselves, through greater size and color-power. Another triangle, inverted, has its base in the row of heads, and its sides converge to the central figure's feet, one man's arm being elongated to define it. From the same base a longer angle comes down to the lower men's knees, there to branch out again. On this firm basic pattern, El Greco as usual imposes an irregular, vibratory movement of the individual parts. Its effect of internal agitation is increased by the close-packed crowding of the figures. Its direction is irresistibly upward, in a flame-like swirl, back and forth in wide sweeping angles at the bottom, then upward in shorter angles, pressed together, trembling and flickering along arms, necks and faces that are twisted by writhing flames and shadows, up to the line of ecstatic faces crowned with literal tongues of flame.

GOYA. THE MAJA NUDE. (*Fig. 36; No. 742.*)

All of Goya's portraits (this represents a duchess of the Spanish court) are strikingly real and individual. They are different in this regard from his decorative paintings, such as *Blindman's Buff* and *Girl and Muffled Men,* which are frankly artificial, whimsical fantasies, more in the style of the eighteenth century French. At the same time, they never lose a certain lightness and delicacy of touch. Like Velazquez, Goya proved that vivid realism need not be heavy, ugly or coarse-fibred. When, as in his portrait of *King Charles IV and his Family,* physical ugliness, flashy pomp, the signs of gross dissipation, stupidity and awkwardness are the essential attributes of his subject, he reveals them with penetrating honesty. We cannot say how much he heightened these qualities, but the net result is devastating satire, all the more piercing for being subtle — as, for the sake of prudence, it had to be.

When, as in *The Maja Nude,* reality itself is physically charming, finely textured and softly voluptuous, he sets down these qualities with equal vividness. It is not exact representation, but selective artistry, to bring out as he does here the essential traits that give this figure its unequalled sensuous allure: its delicate, rich smoothness, and its firm, slender roundness. The body is made to stand out distinctly from its triple background of pillows, couch and wall, as the climax to a series of rising accents in color and modelling. The wall is flat, dull gray-brown; the couch intenser blue-green, with but a hint of roundness in the velvet folds. The pillows and sheet are painted as cloth had never been painted before, in sketchy strokes of white over blue, that convey with utmost reality the filmy diaphanous quality of lace and gauzy silks. In the *Maja Clothed,* the companion piece, this interest in filmy cloths is developed into a bright pattern of

FIG. 36. THE MAJA NUDE
By Goya

orange, green and rose veils, crushed into countless small transparent folds over a skin that is also more warmly colored. Here there is less pattern, less brilliance; the climax is given in the shape and texture of the body itself. It is drawn with unnatural lightness, seeming to float on the lace, in a pose that suggests no weight or muscular strain. Its curves are more deeply indented, quickly rising and falling, than in the Ingres or Giorgione reclining nudes, but softer and rounder than in Manet's angular *Olympia*. It owes much to Titian and Rubens in its modelling with rich blended tints, and this accounts for a large portion of its charm as contrasted with the hard wooden flesh of the Ingres, or the plastery pink and white of an ordinary Boucher. But it is less robust, more delicate and sinuous than the figures of Titian or Rubens. The pale suffusion of blue in the shadows and veins, and the background notes of blue in the lace and velvet, do much to create this distinctive quality of airy lightness and translucency.

GOYA. THE SHOOTING. (*Fig. 37; No. 749.*)

From Goya's late style all trace of gaiety has vanished, and all sensuous delight in lovely textures. Bitter resentment has made him a savage, ironic satirist. The subjects are *macabre*, nightmarish or cynically witty. The expressions are of fear, hatred, or mirth that is grotesque and leering. The most fantastic of these pictures are merely drawn or etched in dark gray or brown ink, sometimes with touches of lurid color. Bodies are gray smudges and streaks against black night, producing sunken, grimacing features and twisted limbs. El Greco's late, distorted style is exaggerated, in flat, broad, extremely simplified strokes. *Saturn Devouring his Children* (763), typical of this period, is all in black and white except for a streak of red blood. The ghastly light

FIG. 37. THE SHOOTING

By Goya

reveals a striking pattern of legs and fists clutching the child's small vertical body. Compared to these, the nightmares of Bosch (in the *Escorial* near Madrid), or those of Félicien Rops, are child's play.

The Shooting was made a few years earlier than most of these. It is less extreme in style, and a fully developed painting. Through being less obviously fantastic, it acquires an even greater power of stark, gripping terror. The colors are appropriate: drab grays and browns against a black, starless sky. It is lighted only by the glare of a lantern on a white shirt and a pool of crimson blood. There is no grace of line, or decorative pattern: only the contrast of one group killing and one being killed. The rhythm is jerky, stiff, staccato, of broad blunt limbs in V-shaped angles; of men on one side lunging in military unison, on the other in a mad confusion, sprawling, cowering, flinging out despairing arms, or clapping hands to eyes. A smudge of gray to show a mouth distorted, another to show one fallen open, a stubby clenched hand, two lines to show a sagging knee — each of these brief strokes tells the story of what is happening. This is terse illustration of the most economical and powerful kind. Inspiring it, and breathing through it, is passionate indignation at this event of 1808, and at what it stood for in the history of his country.

Briefer Mention

EL GRECO. More intensive study should take note of the three different periods in his life. An example of the first is the *Trinity* (824) — comparatively realistic in its solidly modelled figures, and comparatively superficial in its bright pattern of light, clear colors. The portraits of this period are also realistic, with healthy coloring, little distortion, soft even shadows, and accessory objects such as swords and books represented in detail. For example, *A Doctor* (807); *Gentleman with Hand on Breast* (809). The second period mingles realism with distortion, as in the *Resurrection* (825), with bizarre foreshortenings. Portraits, such as *Unknown Man* (813) dispense with nearly all accessories, and produce fantastic designs by livid coloring, by distorting the features themselves with heavy, jagged shadows in depressions of the temples and cheeks. Oddly enough, in the last period, when religious pieces like the *Pentecost* are most fantastic, the portraits return to realism — for example, in three entitled *Unknown Man* (810, 811, 812). Did his noble patrons demand better likenesses, and did he acquiesce because imaginative subjects were affording a freer outlet for experiments in form?

VELAZQUEZ. There is less difference between the early, middle and late works. In the first, *The Drinkers* (1170) reveals his characteristic flattening, smudging abbreviation of unaccented parts, bringing into strong relief the lighted head of the god. It is in dark, autumnal browns, reds and golds. In the middle years he makes more use of fresh, clear, daylight blues, greens and whites, and is less daring, more conventional in subject and form. *The Lances* (1172) is apt to be felt as a rather banal, academic piece of exact representation, until one realizes that much imitation has made it so. Its fresh, gay coloring is, however, more original than its design of spears and soldiers. The third period is most versatile of all, with much specialization; each picture carries some technical problem to its logical extreme. *The Buffoon Pernia* (1199) is an extreme of simplification into flat, broad color-planes, in light vermilion and gray, somewhat like the best Chinese mortuary portraits. *The Idiot of Coria* (1205) is nearest to Rembrandt, in its dark greenish, melting shadows and soft glowing yellow lights. *Moenippus* (1207) is radically distorted, with compressed, elongated features and sprays of repeated curves. *Mariana of Austria* (1191) is his most gorgeous design of rich, realistic textures, in full splendor of rose and gold silks against dull black and silver-gray. *Mercury and Argos* (1175) is the most simplified and sketchy, blurring all details in a swimming mist of thin reds and browns, but leaving a firm rhythmic foundation of solid limbs.

Other Spanish Pictures

RIBERA, *Martyrdom of St. Bartholomew* (1101) — less given than usual to imitating Caravaggio's exaggerated, glaring lights and murky shadows; vigorous in unclassical realism, and in its striking design of outstretched arms and ropes. ZURBARAN, *Visions of St. Peter Nolasco* (1236) — flashily theatrical chiaroscuro, and loose design, but better surface texture in highlights than Ribera's. MURILLO, *Jesus and John as Children* (964) — the soft, sentimental prettiness of the subject is supported here by better coloring than in his early works; the distinctively delicate, opalescent atmosphere is pleasing in itself.

Works of Other Schools

TITIAN, *Self-portrait* (407); *Charles V* (410); *Danaë* (425); *Entombment* (440); *Christ Bearing the Cross* — all late works of highest rank. DÜRER, *Self-portrait* — early and unusually colorful in gray-green, black and gold. CORREGGIO, TINTORETTO, LOTTO, VERONESE, RUBENS, BRUEGHEL, PATINIR, BROUWER, BOSCH, CRANACH, POUSSIN and CLAUDE LORRAIN are all represented by first-class examples.

TOLEDO

Scattered through a dozen churches, in this ancient town of dwindled population, are some of the greatest works of EL GRECO. Some are well preserved and easily accessible, like the *Burial of the Count of Orgaz* in the Church of Santo Tomé. This example of the second period is interesting in that it combines his realistic and fantastic styles in the same picture; one below, in a group of living men, and one above, to represent angels and deities — a contrast similar to that in Tintoretto's *Last Supper* (Fig. 63). Many of the finest works are not in the *Greco Museum* or in the *Cathedral,* but must be sought in small, unused churches in side streets, where some are fast mouldering away. The latest and most fully characteristic are the *Assumption* (Church of San Vicente), *St. Francis* (Hospital of Tavera), *Annunciation* (Church of San Nicolas) and *Adoration of the Shepherds* (Santo Domingo el Antiguo).

The first of these, the *Assumption,* carries his distinctive tendencies to their fullest realization in all his work. A small cloud of flowers at the bottom is the only realistic material left, and even such delicate substance falls solidly and heavily by contrast with the ethereal forms of the Virgin and angels. The last factor to make for stable firmness — the regular, symmetrical basic design noted in the *Pentecost* — is itself melted in the flames, dissolved and swept upward in the rising, fluttering stream of fiery vapors. Almost the last vestige of realism in bodily proportions is gone. Far more than in the *Pentecost,* these figures are dehumanized by tremendous elongations, which seem to give them supernatural size, and at the same time carry up the whole group's movement in great soaring, swerving flights, one above another. In between are finer tresses of crumpled, iridescent drapery, and twisted small angelic figures, all flaring and flickering upward like wisps of burning vapor blown by a whirlwind, to circle at the top in a vortex of luminous clouds. The colors aid this movement vigorously. A greenish yellow, in the lowest angel's dress, is most opaque and nearest to the landscape colors below. Rising, the figures gleam in crimson and lemon-yellow against a sky of dull gray blues and greens.

THE ESCORIAL

This grim, enormous tomb of dead kings and queens contains a small art gallery: the *Capitulary Rooms*. In it is one of EL GRECO's most brilliantly colorful works, a *San Mauricio* of lurid blue-greens, yellow, purple and rose (second period). Near a second-rate VELAZQUEZ, there is an unusually vigorous ROGER VAN DER WEYDEN *Deposition*. Scattered in various rooms through the building are several characteristic works of BOSCH.

CHAPTER IV

ITALY

THE preëminence of Italy in the world of pictorial art was undisputed from the middle ages to the seventeenth century. During that time and ever since, the fruits of those bountiful years have been eagerly sought by all the nations of the earth. To see Italian art, one does not have to go to Italy, for it is in every museum. But away from home it is detached, uprooted. No one can grasp it with full sympathy who has not walked the narrow streets of Florence and glided past Venetian palaces, entering the dim churches and the banquet-halls for which it was produced, and which were themselves products of the same mysteriously transitory age of creative genius. Much of the best remains in its museums, in spite of centuries of exportation. Forever immovable, in particular, are the frescoes, which include many of the greatest works, and which are painted directly into the walls themselves.

The wide distribution of these important frescoes through Italy makes it necessary for the art student to travel more extensively there than in any other country. Even the smaller, detachable pictures are scattered through local museums from one end of the country to the other; there is no such concentration as exists in England, France and Spain. The list of towns and even villages which possess old pictures taxes even the encyclopedic Baedeker, and only a few of the most outstanding will be mentioned in this chapter.

There is of course no one necessary route to follow. Most people go directly to Florence, then to Rome or Venice, and if one's time is short that is the wisest plan. Otherwise there is a geographical advantage in following a fairly straight course from north to south or in the opposite direction, stopping off as many times as possible along the way. The route suggested here begins in the south, at Naples, in order to follow more closely the general chronological order of the principal works to be seen. At Naples and at Rome are the ancient Roman paintings, and at Assisi are the early Giottos. Venice, in the north, represents the culminating phase of Italian art.

NAPLES

The mistaken belief is still widespread that ancient painting was crudely primitive, and that naturalistic painting appeared for the first time when the Madonnas of Cimabue and Giotto relaxed a little from their medieval stiffness. To anyone who holds this belief, a trip to Naples will be a revelation. For the latest and greatest stage of ancient painting, one must go to Rome itself. But here at Naples (in the National Museum) the collection of Roman pictures is much larger, and shows a greater variety of different styles.

Most of the examples here were made as wall-frescoes in Pompeii and Herculaneum. Fortunately (from our viewpoint at least) they were buried suddenly but gently under ashes in the eruption of 79 A.D., thus escaping more thorough destruction in the long decline and fall of the Roman Empire. Most Pompeian art was probably made by imported Greek artists, or in direct imitation of Greek art. But the

FIG. 38. THESEUS AFTER KILLING THE MINOTAUR
Ancient Roman

great native works of Greek naturalistic painting (by Zeuxis and Apelles) are lost; so it is hard to say how much, if any, improvement on them was made by Roman artists, or by later Greeks on Roman soil. However, disregarding all questions of chronology and credit due, it is possible to arrange the works preserved here in order of the complexity of pictorial form which they reveal.

(1) Relatively simple are two paintings in cinnabar on marble, representing *Theseus Delivering Hippodamia from the Centaur* and *Women Playing with Astragali*. These are little more than monochrome line drawings, very similar to those on late Greek vases. Shadows are barely indicated in the former, but the outlines skillfully suggest muscular solidity and rhythmic gesture. No depth is suggested except in the overlapping of limbs to show that one is in front of another. (Fig. 41, the *Pasiphae* at Rome, is a more broadly executed example of this type.)

(2) The second type includes the large majority of surviving Roman paintings. It is essentially an imitation of sculpture, with a few distinctively pictorial elements added. Except for differences in medium and subject-matter, this type corresponds on the whole to Florentine painting in the middle of the fifteenth century: in particular to the work of Verrocchio. The figures are strongly modelled by naturalistic cast shadows. They are statuesquely draped or nude, with limbs and muscles accurately and emphatically rounded. Postures are animated, but often inclined to be rather pompously affected, or gently graceful, in the manner of Hellenistic sculpture. (Compare the statues in this museum.) The principal figures stand out with unnatural sharpness from their backgrounds. Colors and textures emphasize naturalism rather than decorative pattern, but as a rule are too hard, superficial and monotonous to be either rich or deeply realistic. There are fairly convincing glows

of bright sunshine, but no subtle blends to form an atmosphere.

Pictures of this general type show much individual difference. In some, late Greek statues are almost exactly copied, with only flesh-tints added. (E.g., *The Three Graces*.) There is little or no depth in these: either a plain black or red wall surrounds the figures, or there is a slight hint of rocks or flowers just behind them. Some Pompeian decorations of this type (e.g., *Bacchante* and *Flora*) are very delicately modelled, with filmy drapery well suggested in light pastel tints of lavender and yellow.

In others of the same general type the composition and coloring are more complex than would be possible in sculpture, and space is a little deeper. There are many figures, at different distances, going back some ten or twenty feet into imaginary space. At that distance are sunlit walls in fairly accurate perspective, trees and horses as well as people. They are painted more broadly than the ones nearby, and often further dimmed with colorful mists of pale violet or green, to give a sense of intervening atmosphere. The famous mosaic of *The Battle of Alexander*, probably copied from a Greek painting, comes under this heading. It is a finely organized design of long straight lances and irregular flowing curves, anticipating similar designs by Uccello, Velazquez (*The Lances*) and Rembrandt (*The Night Watch*). In addition, it is a remarkable piece of action-drawing, vividly expressing the shock and tumult of battle.

THESEUS AFTER KILLING THE MINOTAUR (*Fig. 38.*) is more typical: a simpler group, quite static, and composed in a fashion that has since become conventional. It has a large central mass and smaller masses balancing it on either side, with a few small parallel curves to vary it. The hero's statuesque body stands out too sharply and with eyes too staring to be natural, in dark bronze against a

FIG. 39. HERCULES' SON SUCKLED BY THE HIND
Ancient Roman

sunlit wall. The minor figures are made lighter and less distinct, against dark walls, thus reversing the other contrast. As a design of masses, it is much weaker than Giotto's or Duccio's best. Compared to the *Odyssey* series at Rome (Fig. 42) space is still shallow, and the group at right is a little huddled — characteristics common in Giotto and Duccio. But the softly tinted, atmospheric haze which dims the farther figures, the realistic sunlight which floods the background, the individuality of the rounded faces, and the bodily realism of the hero, lightly poised on his feet (as in Masaccio) are all qualities of Italian Renaissance painting, laboriously redeveloped fourteen centuries after this was painted.

Exquisite details, more strongly unified as design while equally naturalistic, are to be found in other paintings of this type: for example in HERCULES' SON SUCKLED BY THE HIND (*Fig. 39, No. 9008*). The bodies of animal and child, slender and plumply rounded, gracefully curved and angular, flow together in a firm elliptical pattern against a flat background. On this essentially sculptural basis the painter's art appears in the varied tints and textures, all soft and realistic, done in broad simple strokes. The farther limbs are set back in space by a pale opalescent haze. Unfortunately, this detail (like others of its kind) is part of a large, badly composed and vulgarly over-decorated composition, most of it done in a different brush-stroke — as if some tasteless Roman painter had copied it from a Greek original, or some good Greek artist had painted in only this detail. It is in such stray vestiges, perhaps, that we can catch a glimpse of the lost Greek art of painting.

(3) The third and last type, in which painting has entirely ceased to imitate sculpture, and works purely in its own terms, is illustrated in the LANDSCAPE WITH FIGURES (*Fig. 40, Rm. VI*). No muscular, statuesque bodies now

FIG. 40. LANDSCAPE WITH FIGURES
Ancient Roman

dominate the scene. Deep space, filled with rich atmosphere compounded of light and color (the Venetian rediscovery many centuries later) now constitutes the basis of form. It is still rendered in a dry thin fresco medium, lacking the power and subtlety of Venetian oils, and it passes over surface details with less realism of texture. But in other essential respects its world of visual imagery is akin to that of Carpaccio, Claude Lorrain and even the modern impressionists. The technique is extremely broad, rough and sketchy; not crudely so, but with deliberate, quick simplification, comparable to that in landscapes by Tintoretto, Manet and the Sung Chinese.

The scene goes back, not a few feet, but across a wide river to a distant shore and hilltop. Unlike pure impressionist landscape, it is definitely organized by rhythms of mass and space. Its main division is into two diagonal halves: the lower left including the foreground; the upper right the middle and background. In proportion to distance, these are progressively lighter and vaguer, more obscured in a sunny mist of pale opalescent tints, blended rather sketchily through laying thin films of color, one above another, in broad strokes. The mist is nowhere dense enough to confuse the piled-up colonnades and roofs whose straight lines constitute the chief repeated theme. In a zig-zag of angles, one moves into space from the woman and girl silhouetted in the foreground, up to the left along a diagonal rod which one of them carries, to a group of figures on a platform. The straight rods they are carrying point upward to the right, as do the wavy branches of the tree. From the tripod in lower right another long rod, steps and roof-top repeat this zig-zag, a little deeper into space. The long diagonals of a colonnaded pier lead us out over the water to the distant shore, which mounts in an angular hilltop. Linear perspective is quite adequate for the purpose, though not exact. Cast shadows, too, are used without literal exactness, whenever needed to reinforce the movement of lines and planes. The silhouetting of light and dark planes against each other brings the foreground rhythms into strong, clear emphasis.

All these effects, sought after with great difficulty by modern painting, are achieved with such casual brusqueness that one may guess this to be a quick sketch, by some artist who had acquired assurance through long previous work along similar lines. Of the same general type as the *Odyssey* series at Rome, it is obviously by another hand.

[In the National Museum there is also a large gallery of modern paintings (the *Pinacoteca*). With a very few exceptions, such as Titian's *Danaë*, in Room XXIV, these are mediocre.]

ROME

The Vatican

The great pictures of Rome are in the Vatican, with a few important exceptions noted farther along. The enormous papal palace is almost a city in itself, however, and it is easy to spend hours and walk miles there, wasting eyesight in endless corridors full of ornate bric-à-brac. There are three places in it which must be seen without fail: the *Sistine Chapel*, for Michelangelo's frescoes; the *Raphael Rooms*; and the room of *Ancient Roman Paintings*. The first two are near together, and the third is on the way to them. On the way, also, is the *Library*, whose early Christian and medieval manuscript illuminations will appeal to some tastes as the most important of all. The *Greek and Roman vases*, in Rooms V–VII of the *Museo Etrusco*, offer interesting material for comparison with the Roman wall-paintings.

There is a small picture-gallery in another part of the palace, the *Pinacoteca*. It is famous for its RAPHAEL *Transfiguration;* but this is an uneven work, poorly united, with fine details in the upper part, and inferior ones, executed by his pupils, in the lower. Better of their kind are the small Italian primitives in another room: several works in the Byzantine style, a LORENZO MONACO *Life of St. Benedict* (68), and FRA ANGELICO's *Miracles of St. Nicholas* (116).

ROMAN (ANCIENT). PASIPHAE AND THE BULL. (*Fig. 41.*) THE ALDOBRANDINE WEDDING.

The flood of tourists in the Vatican passes by this inconspicuous, little advertised room, called the *Cabinet of Antique Paintings,* on the right of the long corridor in the Library. It contains a most extraordinary treasure: the *Odyssey* series of Roman frescoes. Far from being primitive, they represent an advanced stage of development rarely equalled in the present day. Although known to connoisseurs, their merits have never been sufficiently appreciated, and histories of art give them nothing like the emphasis they deserve.

Some other Roman frescoes in the room should be noted for the sake of comparison. These correspond to the first and second types mentioned in the section on Naples. *Pasiphae and the Bull* belongs to the first or linear type, since it is essentially an outline drawing, like those on certain late Greek vases. It is in a monochrome of brown, except for a slight film of blue over the dress. Shadows are barely suggested, and the figures are comparatively flat, against a flat, plain wall. The form is simple; but that fact should not be taken as meaning that it is necessarily inferior in quality to pictures with solid modelling in deep space. What it tries to do, it does with forceful directness, in a way that suggests the drawing of such present-day

FIG. 41. PASIPHAE AND THE BULL
Ancient Roman

artists as Picasso. With the most economical means, it is effective both as representation and as design. By the outline alone, it gives a realistic sense of the heavy bulk and strength of the bull, and of the girl's slender lightness. The lines are sufficiently varied in breadth and thickness to avoid monotony, and they combine to form a rhythmic pattern of long diagonals and short curves.

The famous *Aldobrandine Wedding* belongs in form to the second or sculptural type. A long row of statuesque figures, roundly modelled, stands in space against a nearby wall. They are rather a series of separate figures than a composition, since no definite pattern of line or color connects them. Lighting and coloring are fairly naturalistic, but of no great subtlety or depth.

ROMAN (ANCIENT). THE ATTACK OF THE LESTRIGONI (*Fig. 42*) AND OTHERS OF THE ODYSSEY SERIES.

The third or pictorial type comes to full complex development in the *Odyssey* series, of which an example is reproduced. (Lacking color, the illustration gives a very inadequate notion of it.) Similar in general to the *Landscape with Figures* at Naples, it is more monumental in plan, and more rich and subtle in detail. It also includes the element of represented action, lacking in the other, and a more animated rhythm of line and mass. Involving genuinely deep space, and an atmosphere merging light and color, it reveals a mature command of the painter's art, and anticipates many of the greatest achievements of Chinese, Renaissance and modern painting.

The series is connected by a painted framework of architectural pilasters, and by continuous internal themes of form and narrative. Aided by contrast with their frames (flat, bright red and gold on purplish gray) the panels recede into far-off depths of cool blue-green surf and rocky, misty shore. Small, energetic human figures, ships in harbor, houses, trees and animals among the crags, are swept lightly into being with deft, sketchy, simplified strokes. There is no hint of sculptural rigidity or hardness; nothing stands out sharply. Every object takes its definite place in space, and is bathed in the same rich, diffused and variegated atmosphere. Cast shadows are used when needed for the design, to round a shape into solid emphasis, or to spread contrasting films of darker color against the lighter. The incidents from Homer are dramatized clearly enough, but neither human figures nor their actions dominate. The basis of the form in each case is landscape, and into it (as in Brueghel and Claude Lorrain) the people fit as incidental factors, to fill the space with visually interesting forms. Scenery and objects unnecessary to the story receive as much emphasis or more. In other words, the Homeric poem is not merely illustrated, but used as a theme for free imaginative development in pictorial terms. The arrangement of forms is always rhythmic, including only shapes and colors that repeat a few definite themes. But the designs thus made are loose and casual, free-floating and irregular, never tightly obvious.

The Destruction of Ulysses' Fleet consists of three contrasting themes: the angular, strenuous figures of the attacking giants in the foreground; the ships with high curving prows, in a line that leads out to the open sea; and the rocks that circle the harbor. Many small straight lines of wreckage, oars and yard-arms form a minor theme, and all appear against a background of sea and sky. The atmosphere is delicate and rich, blended of many tints and enlivened with strong contrasts. Its pearly opalescence, its colored shadows, anticipate modern impressionism, but without loss of spatial clarity. A ruddy purple with greenish gold, the reflection of sun on nearby rocks and men, fades to silvery lavender and pale blue in the distance. In the shadowy places a deep purplish gray (underpainted with reddish brown in the men) contrasts with the blue-green sea.

The Fleet Approaching Circe's Island. In the next picture vigorous action gives way to a broad expanse of rugged cliffs and harbor: dark blue-green water streaked with silvery light, between the rose-purple cliff on the left and the greenish-gold shore at the right. Three delicate figures at the right form a stately pattern like those of Puvis de Chavannes. Behind them the shore is a hazy, translucent alabaster of white and violet, with broad strokes of green for the rocky contours. The painting is extremely thin, with the whiteness of the plaster shining through films of dry cool color. It gives to fresco as a medium the distinctive charm of water-color, with greater power.

Ulysses in the House of Circe. Here architecture takes the place of cliffs as the dominant background feature. A cool, faintly violet light softens the texture of massive rectangular towers, turning to deeper rose and purple, with greenish glints, in the shadowy portal. (The coloring here suggests Renoir.) Around the static building are a few shadowy forms of trees and people, curved into a gently flowing pattern. Leafage is simplified into a few soft, bristling smudges, in the Chinese manner. The various shades of darkness, and the placing of a few slanting sticks in the ground, mark off spatial intervals with a delicate lightness also suggestive of Sung landscape.

The Attack of the Lestrigoni. (*Fig. 42.*) Here a quick, back-and-forth motion dominates. The rock forms are smaller and more broken; the trees (again simplified in the manner of Chinese landscape) echo the lines and colors of the human figures, and all dart this way and that in a lively rhythm. As in a Pieter Brueghel, the small figures, though apparently dispersed, are all related to each other and to the

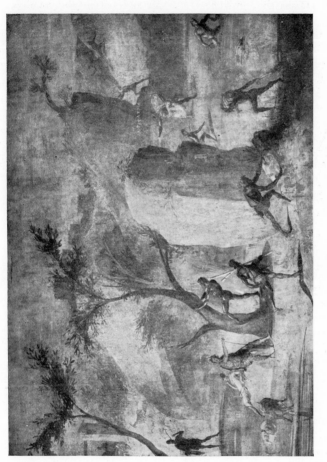

FIG. 42. THE ATTACK OF THE LESTRIGONI
Ancient Roman

landscape, through repeated shapes and systematic grouping, in lines that wind through space at rhythmic intervals. There is great variety in color and lighting. The tranquil design of men and goats under the tree is lightly modelled in violet and reddish brown against a rich glow of yellowish and bluish green, which distinguishes them and the tree from the purple rocks behind. The extreme left of the picture shows deft but unobtrusive skill in light and shade. Distant and subordinated, the figures of man, tree, goat and house with people are flatly silhouetted in various densities of reddish purple, against a pale light that merges in the distance with the deep violet of vague hilltops, bushes and houses, and the blue-green of the sky.

MICHELANGELO. THE CREATION OF MAN; THE FALL OF MAN; AND OTHER FRESCOES IN THE SISTINE CHAPEL. (*Figs. 43 and 44.*)

The Titanic genius of Michelangelo dominates this plain rectangular hall, overshadowing a row of capable frescoes by Perugino, Botticelli and other celebrated painters. On first entering from a narrow passage this room whose walls and ceiling are spread thick with paintings, one feels a sense of bewilderment, in straining to distinguish the figures from each other, and to grasp the plan of their arrangement. One tries to take in at once a whole gallery of different pictures, barely separated by painted architectural borders. Scores of huge bodies are swirling and twisting this way and that, forcing the observer to crane his neck at a dozen uncomfortable angles.

Little by little this feeling of confusion can be diminished, if one studies out the arrangement of the paintings and their relation to the shape of the ceiling itself. Taken all together, they form a single gigantic design, composed of definite units

repeated and alternated. Along the center of the ceiling is
a row of rectangles, alternately large and small, each containing a separate group of figures. These are related in
subject-matter as Biblical scenes of the Creation, the Fall of
Man, and the Flood. They are separated by small decorative
nudes, mostly Greek and Bacchanalian in spirit, one at each
corner of the smaller rectangles, with a medallion between
each pair. Large triangular sections at each corner of the
ceiling, and small ones along the sides, form a contrasting
series of shapes; they represent Old Testament scenes and
characters. Between the triangles, on the pendentives of the
vaulting, there extends around the room a long row of
Prophets and Sibyls, heroic in size, symbolizing the religious
spirit of the Hebrews and other ancient peoples. Each figure
sits in a separate architectural niche, with smaller decorative
figures around and behind it. By taking a broad sweeping
view with half-shut eyes, one can see the whole ceiling as a
single decorative carpet, harmoniously tinted in soft dull
gray-blues, violets and tans, composed of regular geometrical panels, with innumerable small, rounded bodies twined
among them.

But to look at the pictures as mere surface decoration is
to miss the invigorating thrill of those feelings of powerful
effort which they can stimulate in us through suggestion.
Having distinguished the figures as groups, we now see
that they form several independent systems of gravitational
pull. The central rectangular pictures are all organized in
one direction, down the hall toward the altar, where they
pass (through the cleverly foreshortened figure of Jonah)
into the downward torrent of the Last Judgment. Others
along each edge are to be looked at as continuous with the
other walls. It is the close interpenetration of the ceiling
figures that makes these arrangements hard to grasp at first.

Going on to look at each section individually, one feels

FIG. 43. THE CREATION OF MAN

By Michelangelo

with cumulative force that quality of dynamic power which
was evident from the start. But it is gradually seen to be
organized into one stately, majestic rhythm, not a chaotic
mêlée. This effect could not have been produced merely by
large size, big muscles and sweeping gestures. Many later
Baroque pictures, imitating these attributes, succeeded only
in looking bombastic. It is due rather to the fact that each
section is a different design of moving masses, distinct from
all the others, yet fitting into the general flow. The *Libyan
Sibyl* with her open book is a zig-zag of long straight masses;
God Separates Light from Darkness is all short swirling
curves. *The Fall of Man* is balanced in stable symmetry, and
flows in a single rhythm of slender, sinuous, rippling muscles,
beginning in the snake's long body coiling around the tree,
and branching right and left through the two pairs of figures.
The *Creation of Woman* is a criss-cross of lumpish, full
masses in angular diagonals. In the *Creation of Man* a
crescent-shaped form is repeated, and the relaxed, static body
of Adam is contrasted with the whirling cloud of tense
bodies in the opposite corner.

Each separate Prophet, Sibyl and decorative nude is a complex system of masses, in which each limb, head, trunk and
section of drapery acts as an individual unit. They thrust
and counter-thrust in all directions, reaching out, gesturing,
grasping, leaning, swerving, tensely unstable or firm in a
moment of balanced equipoise. Partly each figure maintains
its balance by some extended or supporting limb; but in the
main it is a structure that would fall at once if composed of
dead materials. One feels it to be held together only by an
internal cohesive force — a human will — that impels and
controls every fibre. Violent effort may strain every muscle
(as in the Prophet Jonah and some of the decorative nudes),
or the body may be partly relaxed (as in the drunken Noah
and the Prophet Jeremiah); it may be agitated like Daniel

FIG. 44. THE FALL OF MAN

By Michelangelo

or serene like the Delphic Sibyl. But in the ceiling figures
— not in the *Last Judgment*, where they fall pell-mell —
there is no body and no part of a body that is quite flaccid,
nerveless or unbalanced; each contributes to the dynamic
interplay of forces.

This is the painting of an architect, to whom art is essentially the arrangement of masses; also of a sculptor, to
whom the most interesting masses are those that make up
the human body, with their infinite variety of shapes and
surfaces, curved and angular, flexible and rigid, softly
rounded or full of hard muscular swellings and hollows.
The arrangement of masses in architecture tends on the
whole to be simple, repetitious, symmetrical, obviously balanced, static. But here is a profusion of irregular, swerving,
mobile equilibria, animated from within and bursting strenu-
ously out from the frozen marble that is represented behind
them.

It is also the painting of a poet and a man of humanistic
learning, to whom bodies are not mere decorative shapes,
but beings inspired by human and divine passions and ideas,
which they can be made to convey in attitude and gesture.
Almost every conceivable position of the body is represented
here, it would seem, and each expresses dramatically some
definite state of emotion or will. All the figures — except,
again, in the *Last Judgment*, which is full of savage distorted
caricatures — belong to some race of demi-gods, superhuman
in strength and in majestic freedom of movement. They
inherit the Greek tradition of physical grace, but with more
rugged force. Along with classic naturalism, they express
adequately, for the first time in pictorial art, the epic sweep
of the Old Testament, its pageant of stirring events and its
intense moral fervors.

Is this the painting of a painter? The charge is often
made that Michelangelo is merely a sculptor working in an

uncongenial medium. The taking over of sculptural effects is obvious in the modelling and arrangement of the bodies, and many of them could be effectively rendered in relief or in the round. Nearby spatial intervals are clear, but distant space is not attempted, except in *The Flood;* for it would have complicated an already complex problem, beyond all bounds. The coloring is not rich or subtle, but it has an agreeable dry, light fresco quality, and it helps distinguish the figures, especially the living from the sculptured ones. Light and shade are well used to bring out the relations of masses. Sculpture itself is always more or less at the mercy of changing shadows, and of the spectator's point of view. But here all these are fixed in the right positions as only a painter can fix them.

RAPHAEL. THE SCHOOL OF ATHENS. (*Fig. 45.*) PARNASSUS; THE DISPUTATION; THE MASS OF BOLSENA; THE DELIVERANCE OF ST. PETER FROM PRISON; THE CONFLAGRATION OF THE BORGO.

The walls of these small chambers, called the *Stanze di Raffaello,* show the final stages of Raphael's fast but short-lived progress. Seen in chronological order, they reveal how steadily he was outgrowing those faults for which modern critics have denounced him, and, learning intelligently from his contemporaries, was extending his command over pictorial form. Gone, or fast disappearing, are the bland, insipid, smiling faces of his early Madonnas, the mincing, languid postures of Perugino's saints, the facile swirls of line, the monotonous pyramidal designs, and the hard superficial coloring. Instead, a little of the soft richness of the new Venetian coloring is captured; designs become refreshingly irregular, bodies are more vigorous, linear rhythms are more briskly varied, and faces are more severely, unsentimentally

FIG. 45. THE SCHOOL OF ATHENS
By Raphael

modelled. In particular, there is a steadily growing power of composing many solid figures into complex designs in deep space.

In the *Stanza della Segnatura*, the earliest of these rooms, the *Parnassus* is still full of simpering smiles and affected, theatrical gestures, which repel modern taste in spite of the decorative charm of a dancing, lilting flow of line. Both this and the *Disputation* are rather tiresomely symmetrical, especially the latter, with its obvious theatrical pattern of converging spokes and semi-circles, neatly fitted together in three tiers. But the individual figures are drawn with more spirited, varied attitudes and faces, in a more interestingly broken rhythm of line. Even the neat symmetry of pattern, one should add, is not necessarily a fault, but only uncongenial to the modern spirit. It expresses rather the Greek love of perfect, balanced proportion, and the medieval conception of a small, unchanging, ordered universe of heaven and earth.

But Raphael was sensitive to the restless, experimental spirit of his time, and little by little his designs express this altered mood. *The School of Athens*, done shortly after the *Disputation*, resembles it in being basically symmetrical, and in being built up of long straight lines, semi-circles and swirls that converge and recede toward the center. But its interrelation of parts is less obvious, tight and static; more irregular and animated. The earthly philosophers that people its steps are more diffusely and casually scattered, as separate individuals, or as detached small groups with various objects of interest. Their main outlines still flow together in undulating unison, but with still more variety and dissymmetry in detail. Each has a more roomy bit of space to move in, and the whole group lives in a wider atmosphere of spacious arches and rotundas. Faces and attitudes are vigorous, expressive, diverse. Some are still the typically Raphaelesque ideals of lithe, hard-muscled youth — statuesque, graceful, regular in feature; but the monotony of too much perfection is now prevented by many other faces, ruggedly irregular. In short, the picture still has enough of Raphael's early charm and suavity to please without cloying, along with a mature command over expressive, rhythmic figure-drawing and dynamic, unified deep-space design.

The later pictures show him experimenting boldly with a variety of new effects, moving always away from academic tightness and over-sweetness toward the austere and unconventional. *The Mass of Bolsena* (in the *Stanza di Eliodoro*), though conventional in pattern, contains some of his richest painting of colors and textures. The *Deliverance of St. Peter from Prison* is full of daring lights and shadows, of angular, foreshortened figures, steel-clad, reflecting in fantastic glows and glitters a radiance that comes at once from torch-light, from a lurid sky without, and from angelic auras in a darkened cell. In the *Stanza dell' Incendio* we pass to the pictures executed by other hands from Raphael's designs. As one might expect, their interest lies principally in the composition, the execution of lighting and textures being baldly monotonous. The *Conflagration of the Borgo* shows him venturing into the field of Michelangelo with powerfully knotted, straining nude bodies, and foreshadowing Tintoretto with a bizarrely unsymmetrical design, intricately subdivided into planes at various angles in space. In the frescoes in the *Sala di Costantino*, whatever Raphael contributed through preliminary sketches is lost in the pretentious vulgarity of his followers who executed them.

The Borghese Gallery

In rooms IX and X are three notable paintings; the rest, including a RAPHAEL *Entombment*, can be passed over rapidly. One of the three is CORREGGIO's *Danaë*, with a girl and Cupid arranged in a striking but rather obvious design of angles, which is brought out emphatically by a strong contrast of light against shadow. The others are TITIAN's: the famous *Sacred and Profane Love*, which is a work of early youth, and the *Education of Cupid*, a much later one. The youthful work seems a little hard and sculptural by comparison with the melting rainbow tints in the other, but only when so compared. In grace of gesture, in surface texture, in the soft atmosphere of its Giorgionesque landscape, it is already finished and mature, and in possession of the essential qualities which he developed in later life.

Other Pictures in Rome

The collections in the *Barberini Palace* and the *Gallery of Modern Art* are not of highest quality. It is more rewarding to seek out the great VELAZQUEZ portrait of *Pope Innocent X* in the *Doria Palace:* a piercing expression of character, and a masterpiece of bold modelling in rich tints of red. At the *Museo delle Terme*, on the second floor, are some ancient ROMAN wall paintings, one or two of which embody the late atmospheric coloring mentioned above. Aside from these, pictorial form can best be studied in the many early Christian and MEDIEVAL frescoes and mosaics in churches throughout the city. The most important of these are *San Clemente, Santa Costanza, Santa Pudenziana, Santa Maria Maggiore, Santa Maria in Domnica, Sant' Agnese*, the *Battistero di Costantino*, and the *Catacombs*. There is a thirteenth century fresco of the *Last Judgment* by CAVALLINI, who influenced Giotto, in *Santa Cecilia in Trastevere*.

ORVIETO, PERUGIA, ASSISI AND AREZZO

These are stopping-off places for a leisurely trip from Rome to Florence and Siena. *Orvieto,* a fantastic walled city perched on a hill in the midst of a plain, contains in its cathedral the best works of LUCA SIGNORELLI, whose dynamic designs of nude muscular bodies were an inspiration to Michelangelo.

Perugia and *Assisi* are close together: the former has a museum of Umbrian primitives, but they are insignificant by comparison with the great frescoes of GIOTTO and his followers in the Convent Church of St. Francis at Assisi. These are earlier than his Padua frescoes, and nearer the Byzantine in their tendency either to fairly strict symmetry or the extreme opposite: to bizarre designs of apparently unrelated parts, which are ingeniously linked together by themes of line and color. They are much restored, but the color, however old, is fresh and clear in dry, pale corals, blues and tans. The compositions are novel and inventively varied. *St. Francis Preaching to the Birds* is the most famous; but these are stronger in design: *St. Frances Supporting the Lateran; St. Francis Restores his Apparel to his Father; St. Francis's Vision of a Palace and Weapons.*

Arezzo contains the greatest frescoes of PIERO DELLA FRANCESCA, another pioneer of the early Renaissance, whose smaller pictures in various museums are sadly faded.

PIERO DELLA FRANCESCA. THE QUEEN OF SHEBA ADORING THE CROSS. (*Fig. 46; Church of St. Francis.*)

The grandeur, simple strength and spaciousness of Piero's conceptions make him a worthy successor to Giotto, and rank him above many contemporaries who occupied themselves with petty decorative details. In contrast with a

FIG. 46. THE QUEEN OF SHEBA ADORING THE CROSS
By Piero della Francesca

temperament like Michelangelo's, Piero is essentially static. His *Battle between Heraclius and Chosroes*, in this series, fails to get into action; but where a more unhurried tempo is called for, there his genius finds itself.

These narrow walls behind the altar then expand to epic proportions. Men and women of stately dignity move forward in a slow procession. Long trailing robes and half-extended arms; long slender necks and slender, branching tree-trunks; the arching head of a horse and the arches of distant hills — these simple curves sway back and forth, up and down, along the line in a tranquil and majestic rhythm. There is no crowding: strong light-and-dark contrasts mark off each individual, placing this one near and that one apart in the group. Faces look ahead, engraved in profile, or outward, sculptured with Phidian breadth, serenity and repose. Upright in their smoothly dropping folds, with no affected swirls of line, they stand with the firmness of statues, but more lightly poised, almost floating in space — less massive than Giotto's figures.

The lofty expanse of sky is an intense, unforgettable blue, not medievally flat, not filled with realistic clouds and haze, but varied a little in tone, so that it seems to recede into infinite distance. Its hue condenses to a deeper turquoise in some of the robes, and its pale dry light descends to reveal every figure with unflickering crystal clarity. It fills both highlights and background with a fresh, cool atmosphere, against which garments of deep red, green and gold stand out here and there in warmer contrast.

SIENA

The *Academy of Fine Arts* contains a large representation of the Sienese school. The works of these artists are most noteworthy: *Duccio, Simone Martini, Lippo Memmi, Pietro* and *Ambrogio Lorenzetti, Giovanni di Paolo, Sano di Pietro* and *Pinturicchio.* In general the earlier are the stronger, in both design and expressive feeling. The later ones run to pretty, insipid faces with Byzantine gilt surface decoration, made while the Florentine painters were accomplishing more substantial things.

The greatest is *Duccio,* and his best work is to be seen in the *Cathedral Museum.* It is a series of twenty-six small panels called *Scenes from the Life and Passion of Christ,* to be found on the back of a rather tiresome, formal altar-piece, *The Madonna Enthroned.* They are full of life and variety in design and movement. Often the Byzantine and Roman styles are combined in the same picture, showing the transition then going on from one epoch to another. The figure of Christ will be done in Byzantine gold and flat color, with stiff conventionalized garment-folds; the others in natural tints with softer drapery and cast shadows. Examples of this are *The Last Supper* and *The Kiss of Judas.*

DUCCIO. THE THREE MARYS AT THE TOMB. (*Fig. 47. Second panel from right, top row.*)

Duccio shares with his younger contemporary, Giotto, the honor of having led painting from the Byzantine style back to Roman naturalism, and thus of having inaugurated the modern epoch. Like Giotto, he combines naturalism with original, well-integrated designs. But his figures have, as a rule, less massive strength than Giotto's, and more gentle, fluent grace. In the picture shown, the four figures are typically slender and supple, with outlines that bend into flowing, repeated curves. (Notice the right side of the angel, and the right hand of the foremost woman). The rhythm thus established is carried on into delicate arabesques of drapery, especially in the angel. There the decorative quality

FIG. 47. THE THREE MARYS AT THE TOMB
By Duccio

of line anticipates Botticelli, though with more restraint. In both the angel and the foremost Mary, there is a quality which Giotto often lacks: that of suggesting the sway and pressure of actual limbs beneath the voluminous drapery; this increases the general effect of life and movement. The faces, however, are more stereotyped in the conventional, uniform Byzantine sadness. In other panels, such as *The Kiss of Judas*, they are given more varied expression.

Though fluent line is a distinctive quality in the picture, it is not emphasized to the point of ornateness, and it is well supported by other pictorial effects. Two other, bolder, linear themes — the straight lines and angles of the tomb, and the jagged mountain range — contrast with the sinuous drapery-curves, and thus invigorate the total design. The dynamic interplay is heightened by distorted perspective in the tomb-cover, which slants upward to the right, off-setting the opposite slant of the angel's arm and the shrinking women. Further life is added by strong light-and-dark contrasts be-tween the figures, and between various planes of the tomb and mountains. The planes thus lighted (side and cover of tomb, and four slanting mountain-sides) are arranged like spokes of a wheel, whose axis is the right hand of the fore-most woman. There is a strong suggestion, in these planes, of an upward, revolving movement out of the tomb, and every outline of the figures contributes to it. Obviously, this movement is in harmony with the resurrection subject. Much fading, and the coming through of green under-painting in the faces, make it hard to imagine the original colors. But surviving traces suggest an approach to natural-ism in the flesh, cloth and stone, along with a more medieval brilliance in the wings, sky and haloes. The flat Byzantine sky does not destroy an effect of spacious grandeur, pro-duced by the dignified slender height of the figures, and the vision of lofty peaks behind them.

[In the *Cathedral Library* are frescoes by Pinturicchio, and book-illuminations by various painters. Most of the latter combine medieval coloring with Renaissance model-ling.]

FLORENCE

The importance of Florence as the artistic capital of the Renaissance and of modern Italy is too well known to need general comment. It contains the largest and most repre-sentative picture-gallery in the country, the *Uffizi*, in addi-tion to several churches and other buildings containing pictures of the highest rank.

The Uffizi

The rooms follow chronological order, on the whole. Many of the most interesting works are in rooms far from the entrance, and as usual we shall mention some of these first. Afterward, briefer mention is made of others in the order of rooms.

BOTTICELLI. THE BIRTH OF VENUS. (*Fig. 48; Rm. VI, No. 878.*)

To look through the first five rooms of the Uffizi, and then stand before this picture and the *Spring*, nearby, is to relive one of the most delightful phases of the Renaissance. It is to leave behind the stiff, lugubrious world of medieval asceticism, and witness again the rebirth of the spirit of Venus in European art. Like the fresh sea-breeze that carries her ashore, there comes again an exhilarating freedom and lightness, a healthy joy in physical life and movement, in the fruit and flowers and open air of this world. Not that

FIG. 48. THE BIRTH OF VENUS

By Botticelli

pagan naturalism is fully revived in these works: there is still far to go before the robust sensuality of Titian and Rubens will be reached. These forms — even the pregnant figure of Spring — are still delicate, restrained, cool and chaste. Not that a sensuous joy in bright color and graceful line was lacking in all the earlier men — one has felt it in passing the works of Lorenzo Monaco and Fra Lippo Lippi. But here that mood is entirely freed from an otherworldly, religious subject-matter, with its attendant limitations on form, and it has frankly devoted itself to recapturing the spirit of late Greek sculpture.

In spite of the obvious debt to Greek art, especially in the figure of Venus, there is a distinctly personal note throughout. It is found especially in the use of line, and whatever appeal the picture has from a standpoint of pure form is mainly linear. Botticelli is one of those artists who twine the outlines of things into a definite, continuous melody that can be followed in itself, without regard to what they represent. He is akin to the Gothic craftsmen, and to those that covered the Mohammedan mosques with abstract tracery, in this love of linear music. But his music is suave and classically simple by comparison with theirs. It is never entirely lost in involved detail: one follows it easily and continuously, beginning in the outlines of the two Zephyrs at the left. One feels a sense of lively movement and of contrast in tracing their long, sweeping wings, their drapery bent into S-shaped curves, their arms and legs almost straight. Their floating, whirling movement is quickened by a clever arrangement of the four legs, so that one tends to see them as successive positions of one leg, raised at the left, dropped to vertical, and raised again at the right — as in a cinema film, or in some futuristic modern paintings. The breath of the Zephyrs, naïvely shown in a straight white line, carries this motion to the goddess, who sways supply before the wind, her hair blown out ahead, as she drifts into the outstretched arms and cloak awaiting her. Over these main contours, and the static ones of shore, trees and shell, there plays a lighter melody of short irregular curves in hair and draperies, in falling roses and in V-shaped wavelets, blowing in the wind, darting and curling into impossible twists and scallops.

This emphasis on linear music has its drawbacks, when it is carried to the extreme of almost separating line from color, light and mass. The motion can never be as powerful as in Michelangelo and Rubens, where the masses themselves are caught up, or in El Greco, where it is conveyed in colors. Here it parts company with these, and winds itself into intricate convolutions of its own, dragging garment-folds and locks of hair into strained, frozen shapes. The total form loses in unity, in realism, and in the quality of well-rounded fullness that it has in Titian. Light and color are static and superficial here; everything is hard and sculptural, as if carved from stone and then covered with a thin layer of gilt and pigment. But, though color does not join the movement, or contribute a rich texture, it is agreeable as a pattern in itself. By comparison, all of Botticelli's other works (including the *Spring*) are dull and drab. This has a fresh, clear, daylight harmony of light blue, rose and white, in the dry, eggshell surface of old porcelain.

GIOVANNI BELLINI. ALLEGORY OF PURGATORY. (*Fig. 49; Second Venetian Room, No. 631.*)

Symbolic meanings, and other specific associations of the subject-matter of pictures, are touched on only rarely and incidentally in this book. They form an interesting study in themselves, like that of the lives of painters. But these studies are very different in aim and method from the direct

FIG. 49. ALLEGORY OF PURGATORY
By Giovanni Bellini

appreciation of pictorial form. If such associations, and the problem of tracing them out through religious and literary history, are kept too much in mind as one looks at a picture, one is apt to miss the more directly, universally enjoyable qualities of the form itself. To understand the symbolism, moreover, gives no basis for appraising the artistic merits of a picture. Artists good and bad use the same subject-matter and the same symbolism; the essential question from the artistic standpoint is how they treat their subject-matter, whatever it is, in distinctive forms of line, light and color.

If this is borne in mind, however, it may also be recognized that conveying certain associations is often an important aim in the mind of the artist, and a considerable source of interest to the spectator. They need not conflict with the enjoyment of form. In many analyses in this book mention is made of associations which are practically universal — such as those of maternal sentiment, physical strength, natural landscape, war and humor. There are other associations which are more recondite, or arbitrarily fixed by convention, such as the symbol each saint carries of his peculiar martyrdom. As one cannot enjoy Dante's poetry to the full without learning some of his basic hidden meanings, so an understanding of pictorial symbolism can be made to enrich one's total enjoyment of pictures where it plays an important rôle.

Without attempting to explain the meanings of Bellini's *Allegory* in detail, we may notice it as an example of how symbolism can be woven into design. The picture is said to illustrate a fourteenth century French religious poem, in which the poet travels like Dante to Purgatory. Every figure is made to express a religious idea: the Madonna praying for the souls, who are shown as children playing; the tree of the Song of Songs, and the leafless Tree of Knowledge; a bunch of grapes, symbolic of Christ, over the

Madonna's head; two saints (Job and Sebastian) interceding; a Centaur in the distance, standing for man's lower nature; a man in oriental dress, the type of unbelievers; a hermit in a cave, showing the austere life which shortens one's stay in Purgatory, and so on throughout the picture.

From the viewpoint of art, again, we must ask whether these meanings are well expressed in terms of painting, as Dante expressed his in melodious verse and graphic images. The same symbols could be mere dead hieroglyphics, but here they are built into a complex, visible world of solid forms in deep space, capable of giving, as one looks, the mystic illusion that one is actually present in that strange twilight limbo of waiting souls called Purgatory. How does Bellini do this in a way that earlier painters had not done and could not have done? Such mastery of deep space composition, combining natural perspective, clear intervals between objects, and intricate rhythms of plane and mass, was most advanced for his day. Masaccio had been dead only about sixty years, and Raphael was still an infant. Most important of all, deep space is for the first time filled, and every object bathed, in the glowing atmosphere of soft golden, ruddy light that became the glory of later Venetian painting. This not only makes the illusion of reality more compelling; it has a mystic effect of its own. Unnaturally clear and distinct, every figure stands motionless in a strange autumnal radiance unlike any actual sunlight, that seems to come out of the brown rocks themselves, and out of the phosphorescent blue-green sky and water.

ANTONIO DEL POLLAIUOLO. HERCULES KILLING THE HYDRA. (*Fig. 50; Rm. V, No. 1478.*)

Violent exertion, the struggle of tense wiry bodies, with muscles clenched in fierce attack; crushing grip and

FIG. 50. HERCULES KILLING THE HYDRA
By Pollaiuolo

agonized resistance; these modes of action are graphically represented with a few outlines and shadows. This interest in realistic anatomy and the portrayal of movement is characteristic of the "scientific generation" in fifteenth century Florence; it led the way for Michelangelo, Tintoretto, and the centuries of later work along that line. Too often it has degenerated into mere illustration, interesting only for the story told. But Pollaiuolo's line is not only tersely expressive of bodily action; it retains a decorative quality, in its play of sinuous curves, that is often lacking in merely realistic art.

Briefer Mention

Room I. CIMABUE, *Virgin with Son* (8343); GIOTTO, *Virgin with Child and Angels* (8344) — both Byzantine in stiff symmetry and gold backgrounds; the Giotto prophesying the Renaissance with more solid modelling, rosier flesh-tints, expressive faces, easier attitudes and more perspective. *Room II.* MARTINI and MEMMI, *Annunciation* (452) — still Byzantine in bright, shallow, non-realistic color-pattern, but a fluent grace of line, and tender, animated feeling in face and gesture. *Room III.* VENEZIANO, *Virgin with Child and Saints* (884) — more naturalistic; faces and bodies more solid, varied, firmly poised; gold omitted, colors still not natural, but less sharply contrasting, in a delicate harmony of pale rose, blue and green. Room *IV.* FILIPPO LIPPI, *Coronation of the Virgin* (8352) — great variety of individualized, realistic faces; problems of deep space attacked in foreshortened drawing and arrangement of figures; some crowding and confusion; color unusually rich and subtle for the Florentine school, with a quiet harmony of soft, variegated, blended tints. *Room V.* VERROCCHIO, *Baptism of Jesus* (8358) — anatomical exactitude replaces decorative design. LEONARDO DA VINCI,

Adoration of the Magi (1594) — unfinished, but dramatic in its bold, irregular, rhythmic curves, and its rugged, unsentimental modelling of strangely shaped, expressive heads. *Room VII.* ANDREA DEL SARTO, *Madonna of the Harpies* (1577) — lacking color-power, and tediously symmetrical, it appeals through sensitively varied shadows and a rhythmic, in-and-out motion of strong, graceful limbs. *Venetian Rooms.* TITIAN, *Reclining Venus* (1437) — a colorful, winsome elaboration of Giorgione's Dresden Venus. MANTEGNA, *Adoration of the Magi* (910) — Venetian painting before its sharp outlines had melted into atmosphere; an intricate, detailed design, with modelling like Roman sculpture, and clear deep-space arrangements. *Baroque Room.* CARAVAGGIO, *The Young Bacchus* (5312) — the decline of Italian painting into photographic representation; lacks his usual faults, bombastic gesturing and exaggerated shadows; prophesies the seventeenth century in its naturalistic subject-matter and its new, bright, varied colors.

The Pitti Palace

Many of its former treasures have been transferred to the Uffizi, but the Pitti is still the best place to see RAPHAEL's easel paintings. Beside the Madonnas mentioned below, it contains *The Veiled Lady* (245), whose sleeve is the most richly colored bit of texture he created; and several strong portraits, especially that of *Pope Leo X and Cardinals* (40). There are portraits by TITIAN and TINTORETTO, and a *Magdalen* (67) by the former. Titian is also credited with at least the central figure in the *Concert* of GIORGIONE.

RAPHAEL. MADONNA OF THE CHAIR. (*Fig. 51; No. 151.*)

As *The School of Athens* marks Raphael's high point in deep-space composition, *Madonna of the Chair* is in several ways his best Madonna and his best easel-picture. To judge its progress over earlier works, there is abundant material here for comparison.

Madonna of the Goldfinch (1447 in the Uffizi) is a typical example of his early, sweetly sentimental style, beloved by the public but anathema to sophisticated tastes. It has nothing to offer but pretty, smiling faces and tender attitudes — no color, no design but the conventional pyramid; a stereotyped, feathery landscape taken from Perugino; drab flesh tints and wooden drapery. *Madonna del Baldacchino* (165 Pitti) is the same thing on a larger scale, developed into a more complex altar-piece of dead, conventional symmetry, bald and insensitive in modelling. It is inferior in every way to Andrea del Sarto's *Madonna of the Harpies* (1577 Uffizi), a formal altar-piece of similar plan. *The Granduca Madonna* of Raphael (178 Pitti) is refreshingly simple and straightforward. It makes no pretense at decorative form at all, but frankly offers its conception of the perfect mother and child, unornamented, against a plain black background. But its modelling with soft shadows is a weaker version of Leonardo, and its ideal face — the bland, seraphic half-smile, the perfect oval countenance on which no earthly passion has left the marks of experience — is interesting chiefly as an expression of the Christian ideal.

Returning to the *Madonna of the Chair* after these comparisons, one finds no radical change, but a considerable enrichment of the form from a visual standpoint. The design is simple but rhythmic, unified and unhackneyed. It is

FIG. 51. MADONNA OF THE CHAIR
By Raphael

essentially a sculptural relief, in shallow space, well adapted to the circular frame. Two U-shaped masses fit together: the mother's head and arm, and the child's whole body. Brighter lighting and garments of yellow, red and green accent these parts and further knit them together. The mother's head is one of a series of smaller, rounded masses, scattered about the edge as a secondary theme; the rest are the other two heads, the mother's blue-clad knees and the chair-back. Duller lighting and coloring subordinate all but the two principal faces. The head of St. John is quite Venetian in surface. The other flesh and cloth textures are still rather hard by Venetian standards, especially the blue, but considerably warmer and richer than in Raphael's early works. In this regard, it is the superior of any of his paintings except *The Veiled Lady* (245 Pitti) and some parts of the *Sistine Madonna* at Dresden.

In addition, it retains the perfect oval faces and the tender sentiment of his youthful work. These are qualities which repel some observers as much as they attract others. But they are less exaggerated here than in his earlier pictures; less so than in the *Sistine* — less artificially simpering; more genuine, mature and restrained. No basic human value like these can be dogmatically condemned in painting. They become undeniable faults only when carried to extremes, and unsupported by a sound basis in form.

FRA FILIPPO LIPPI. MADONNA AND CHILD. (*Fig. 52; No. 343.*)

Here the *tondo* or circular form is made the basis of a complex and unusual design. Unlike Raphael's *Madonna of the Chair*, it is not a shallow sculptural relief, but a vista into deep space. It is intricately fitted together of odd perspectives, of walls at different angles, of contrasting lights

FIG. 52. MADONNA AND CHILD
By Filippo Lippi

and colors, and of figures in different attitudes, at different distances from the eye. The result is a design made up of spatial compartments, quite different from any of Giotto's, and different also from the realistic space composition of the later Renaissance. The individual faces are subordinated to an extent unusual in Lippi, and the picture consequently lacks the popular appeal of some of his others, in which unidealized Florentine visages beam forth amiably. In the arrangement of figures, it is far removed from the confused huddling of his *Coronation of the Virgin* (8352) and from the Byzantine, decorative flatness of the *Virgin Adoring* (8353). Its coloring, too, has lost his early Byzantine quality of bright surface contrasts. The outlines still stand out in linear sharpness, especially in the ornate draperies of the woman with the basket. But the flesh-tints are softer, and the color-areas more closely merged into one pervasive key of dull red, gray-green and golden brown — Venetian in hue, if not in texture.

The sharp distinctness of parts, which would conflict with Venetian atmosphere, is here necessary to bring out the complex design. At bottom, the scheme is a division of the circle into wedge-shaped segments, their points toward the center. But this is never tiresomely exact: the points are all a little off center; the segments irregular and different in size. The most emphatic of these is formed by the Madonna and child, a triangular group, with the Madonna's head, which is the picture's focus, coming above the center of the picture. Another is the whole upper right-hand section, of many light-colored walls, coming down to a point at her left shoulder, again off center. A third is the group about the bed, whose lighted bodies form a triangle pointing toward the Madonna's right cheek. Smaller triangles are found in the red curtains and coverlet, the stairway and lighted parts of the floor. Deep-cut windows and doors, in oblique perspective, floor-tiles and steps, knees and elbows of figures, all fit into this pattern of converging angles.

The Academy of Fine Arts

This gallery has an important collection of Byzantine and Tuscan paintings of the 13th and 14th centuries, and less important Tuscan paintings of the 15th to the 17th centuries. Bernardo Daddi, Orcagna and Lorenzo Monaco are represented by formal altar-pieces.

BYZANTINE SCHOOL. CRUCIFIXION AND STORIES OF THE PASSION. (*Fig. 53; 13th century.*)

Here an expression of suffering is heightened by distortion and simplification to the point of caricature. To the medieval churchman, however, so forcible an aid to realizing the agony on the cross was desirable for religious reasons. It was strikingly obvious, stark and emphatic even from a distance. It acted as a powerful stimulus to emotions of sympathy, gratitude and adoration. Its directly visible qualities at the same time gripped the attention with a more sensuous thrill, and drove home the religious message with the concentrated force of organized design.

This visual appeal can be felt today, apart from any religious associations. Broad heavy lines, which are also strips of contrasting color, weave a tight but graceful arabesque of small repeated curves around the features, the locks of hair, the intricate garment-folds and the stiffly conventionalized muscles and ridges of the body. Within the cramping limits of the traditional crucifix, the artist has achieved a certain vigor in the zig-zag swerve of the body, and in the fluent tracery that winds over it, accented sharply by strong sudden contrasts of light and dark.

The smaller pictures are typically flat, with stiff postures

FIG. 53. CRUCIFIXION
Byzantine School

and set, doleful expressions. Their varied compositions, however, help decrease an otherwise monotonous symmetry. All the parts, including the central figure, made a brilliant display of contrasting colors (now badly faded) against the flat gold background. The latter, burnished and jewelled with oriental splendor, served to reflect the altar lights of some dim, small-windowed thirteenth century church. One should imagine this crucifix there, not detached from its setting and hung in a crowded museum.

BYZANTINE SCHOOL. ST. JOHN THE BAPTIST. (*Fig. 54.*)

A false impression of medieval art, as being monotonously symmetrical, rigid and inexpressive, is held by many persons who have seen only the large formal altar-pieces and apse-mosaics. Such designs were often most narrowly restricted by convention, and by the requirements of a symmetrical architectural setting. It is rather in the works intended for less conspicuous positions — in the small scenes attached to a large Crucifixion or Madonna, in manuscript illuminations, and in other comparatively informal pictures — that one discovers the freedom and variety of which medieval art was capable. One need not study out their recondite symbolism to appreciate them pictorially; too much scholarship has a way of confusing aesthetic vision. Some of them are surprisingly animated, expressive, free, sketchy and individual in drawing. Some are elaborately ornamented, others austerely plain. They represent not only dolefulness, but a wide variety of feelings and actions. They use all manner of color-schemes, linear rhythms and unsymmetrical patterns. The ignoring of natural laws and appearances allows them a free rein for imaginative design, for combining fanciful elements that cannot actually be seen together.

FIG. 54. ST. JOHN THE BAPTIST
Byzantine School

In this *St. John* we have an unsymmetrical design, done in broad, decisive strokes that dart across the picture in a bold staccato of swerving diagonals. As in the setting of an Elizabethan drama, just enough realistic details are given to direct the imagination: rocky crags and trees to suggest the desert; the shaggy, unkempt hair and garment of the Saint; his dead face in the platter, prophetic of the story's end. Facial expressions are tersely indicated, and features and rocks are slightly modelled with colored shadows. That amount of realism is compatible with brusque distortion of line and mass (note the small head) to heighten the formal rhythm, and with an unnaturally brilliant pattern of gold and bright colors. The latter, now much darkened, were swept on in contrasting streaks and dots, layer upon layer, to make an iridescent rainbow display.

Church of Santa Maria del Carmine

Masaccio. The Tribute Money. (*Fig. 55.*)

For five centuries the artists of Europe have come to these frescoes in the Brancacci Chapel, to learn expressive drawing and the use of light and shade. Indebted to Giotto for realistic modelling and gesturing, Masaccio went beyond his master in these respects. Since these were qualities highly prized by the later Renaissance, Masaccio's influence was even stronger.

If we compare *The Tribute Money* with one of Giotto's typical compositions, certain differences are obvious. The Masaccio is less firm and impressive as a design of masses. The figures are more alike in shape, standing upright, heads on the same, monotonous level, against a background mostly upright trees and columns. A few slanting arms and cloth-folds are echoed in the distant hillslopes, to give a contrasting

FIG. 55. THE TRIBUTE MONEY

By Masaccio

theme. But there is nothing like Giotto's inventive variation and architectural building up of complex forms. This is more diffuse and casual: simply a group of people talking. But to compensate, we have in the first place individual figures of considerably more animation, lightness and agility. A notable example is the young man in the center, poised on one slender leg, with the other rising from the ground, his body twisted, head and hands extended with fluent, simple realism. Another is the squatting fisherman at the left; and, in other pictures nearby, those of *Adam and Eve Expelled from Eden*, and the man shivering with cold in *St. Peter Baptizing*.

Still more important, as a fundamental development in form, is the genuinely deep space and the wide dispersion of objects in it. Here is no flat gold or blue background, but a vast landscape, receding hill by hill to a far horizon, clearly marked off at various distances by trees and rocky slopes. Its greens and blues, put in distemper on the finished surface, have suffered badly from fire and damp. Even in a drawing made from it by Ruskin, feathery trees, streaks in the sky and details on the hills appear, which are now invisible. Among the figures, there is no cramped huddling: each is in his own bit of space, with plenty of elbow-room. As to color, it is hard to tell which of its qualities are original, and which due to time and restoration. Dust-gathering irregularities in the wall now help to give a shimmering, foggy look to the landscape. The garments are hard, but form a darkly glowing pattern of red, orange, violet and blue against the dull background.

Notice also the broad, simplified modelling in *St. Peter Healing and Giving Alms*; the soft, enveloping shadows and dramatic contrasts of light and dark, anticipating Leonardo and Rembrandt.

Museum of San Marco

Frescoes and panel paintings by *Fra Angelico*; the latter in the room called the *Ospizio*. Of the former, one of the best is the large *Crucifixion* in the *Capitolo*; others are on the upper floor, in passages and cells.

FRA ANGELICO. THE ANNUNCIATION. (*Fig. 56.*)

"Simple and childlike" are the words most often used to describe Fra Angelico's art, and to account for its wide popular appeal. As far as his method of drawing and painting is concerned, it is rather the opposite of childlike spontaneity, being almost geometrical in its hard-finished precision. (Notice especially the columns and the angel's wing.) This picture is simple in places, and elsewhere packed with fine miniature detail, as in the grass and trees at left. But it does make an appeal to certain childishly simple modes of response in the observer, which are often delightful to experience after too much sophistication and subtlety. Its effects are all very obvious and direct, easily grasped at once, with no complex interrelations to study out. Its colors are akin to those of medieval book illumination: pure, intense and bright, without being barbarously glaring. Enamel-like deep and pale blues, rose and coral pinks, olive and emerald greens, bits of shiny gold, all gleam side by side in a gay display. They are well distributed in spots to make a united pattern, but have little approach to blending of tints: only the iridescent glitter, as in the angel's wing, of small contrasting streaks, such as one finds in Byzantine illumination. Each hue is used, as a rule, in one light and one dark shade, no more. They are quite superficial, hard, uniform within a given area. The use of line, light and space is also obvious and direct. One or two arcs and angles, geometrically plain, are repeated with little

FIG. 56. THE ANNUNCIATION

By Fra Angelico

variation, in a clear-cut outline that is easy to follow, never sketchy or disappearing. Plain highlights and shadows round out columns, faces and garments, and these rest side by side in nearby space; not in too rigid symmetry, but with no complex mutual stresses and strains (as in Giotto) or eccentric movements (as in Tintoretto) for us to follow in imagination. The attitudes are neither stiff nor very energetic, but uniformly gentle, dainty and quiet. Like the faces, they express a few simple, childlike emotions — tenderness, awe, joy and grief — no psychological subtleties. They are pious and unworldly enough to satisfy the religious, while lacking the tortured intensity of Gothic religious art. All these qualities combine to produce a consistent and distinctive form that is charming at first — to sophisticated as well as naïve tastes — but has little power to move deeply or sustain long interest.

Medici-Riccardo Palace

Frescoes by BENOZZO GOZZOLI, in the Chapel; and a Madonna by FRA FILIPPO LIPPI, in the banquet-hall.

BENOZZO GOZZOLI. THE JOURNEY OF THE MAGI. (*Fig. 57.*)

The four walls of the dim little chapel are spread with a gorgeous cavalcade of kings and magi, knights and pages, horses, camels, leopards, apes and falcons, winding in an endless procession through a fabulous landscape, sauntering, gossiping and turning aside to hunt. Coats and bridles of scarlet, blue and gold brocade, crowns, velvets and furs glisten against the cool dark green of trees and grass. There are plump gray horses, slender active grooms, long straight lances and towering lance-like trees with fantastic plumed and many-layered tops, fruit-trees, roads, castles, cliffs and

FIG. 57. THE JOURNEY OF THE MAGI
By Benozzo Gozzoli

blue hills. All these brilliantly decorative themes, in endless variation, are organized without the slightest confusion, monotony or crowding. The design is more comparable to a Chinese landscape scroll than to an ordinary European picture, in that all the walls flow together into one long continuous symphony of repeated shapes and colors, intertwining and unwinding, rising to climaxes and falling again, like the melodies in polyphonic music.

Other Pictures in Florence

These at least should not be missed: the powerfully modelled *Last Supper* by ANDREA DAL CASTAGNO, in the monastery of Sant' Apollonia; the GIOTTO frescoes of the *Life of St. Francis*, in the Church of Santa Croce, badly restored but preserving his basic designs; the GHIRLANDAIO frescoes in Santa Maria Novella, with a pageant of Florentine life in decorative line and intricate spatial perspectives; the frescoes by ORCAGNA in the Strozzi Chapel of the same church, fascinating for their subject-matter, the universe of medieval religion. The *Biblioteca Laurenziana* exhibits ancient, medieval and Renaissance manuscript illuminations.

PADUA

GIOTTO. THE DESCENT FROM THE CROSS (DETAIL). (*Fig. 58; Arena Chapel.*)

This mature work of the principal founder of modern painting is typical in its complex, strongly unified design of masses, and in the dramatic expressiveness of its attitudes and faces. The individual figures are not complex, but the extreme of simplicity, in the sense in which Egyptian sculpture

FIG. 58. THE DESCENT FROM THE CROSS
By Giotto

is simple. They are built of broad, almost unbroken planes, flat curves, and straight edges, with practically no decorative ornament. The two nearer figures, with backs to the observer, are especially massive — as rock-like and unshakable as Egyptian pyramids. The whole picture is simple in its lack of small details, applied decoration, elaborate costumes or background. Nothing is irrelevant to the basic design of masses: even the slight decorative border on some of the garments functions to accent the direction of principal contours. The arrangement of masses, on the other hand, is extremely complex by comparison with many pictures where a basic poverty is concealed by elaborate ornamentation. It produces a total effect of simplicity through its completely united coöperation of parts.

Dramatic interest centers in the head of Christ, and it is here that the organization of lines and masses also comes to a focus. This being off center, the whole design is made unsymmetrical, and therefore more dynamic and mobile than if exactly balanced. Smaller parts gather about this focus, holding the attention: especially the other haloed head bent close, and the three supporting hands. Their fingers, the rays of the haloes, the hair and features of the two heads, all make a tight revolving cluster of small straight lines that acts as a decorative climax to the whole design (analogous to a spot of concentrated color in Cézanne).

Looking outward in all directions, we see how the other forms converge toward it or circle around it. First there is an elliptical ring of six other heads bent toward these two, framing them in. The massively draped bodies lean forward like heavy supporting buttresses. This inner ring of heads and bodies is in turn supported by remoter figures: by the seated woman with long hair (Magdalen) holding Christ's feet; by the bearded man behind her, standing erect as an immovable column; and by the other standing figures on both sides of the central group. A thick wall just beyond these figures holds them compactly in the foreground, and swerves diagonally down to meet the other converging masses at the head of Christ.

The design is so intricate that many other subordinate patterns and internal rhythms can be discerned. For example, the five figures seated or bending low, immediately around the body of Christ, can be regarded as a long flat elliptical group in themselves. Four of them (leaving out the one just behind and supporting Jesus) are more voluminous than the standing figures; their broad full draperies are more brightly illumined, and more smoothly unbroken. The taller, standing figures rise up from behind them like the superstructure on a foundation, their masses made more light and fragile (like Ionic columns) by many small vertical folds in their garments. Again, one can notice the rhythm of angles and triangles around the head of Christ. The two figures seated with backs to the spectator form the base of a triangle, whose apex is the head and shoulders of the figures standing above. The clasped hands and arms of this figure form an angle repeating this apex. Below the back of Christ there is a similar angle in the drapery; it recurs in the elbow resting on Christ's arm; and, much smaller, in the zig-zag of drapery rising above his forehead. The curves and angles of these principal figures are echoed in some outlying objects not shown in the illustration (a dead tree on the rocky slope at right, and weeping angels in the sky) which serve to radiate and diffuse the rhythm gradually into the distance.

GIOTTO. THE RESURRECTION OF LAZARUS. (*Fig. 59.*)

A second picture by Giotto is included, in order to suggest the variety of his designs, and also some of their

FIG. 59. THE RESURRECTION OF LAZARUS
By Giotto

limitations. One cannot look over his frescoes, here or at Assisi, without being impressed by their extraordinary inventiveness. Far from repeating a formula, they present in every case some surprising new arrangement of masses, each fitted together with unerring architecture. Here, for example, there is no converging to a single focus, either of shapes or of dramatic interest. The eye is at once drawn to the striking figure of the risen man, swathed, cadaverous, but unmistakably alive within his shroud. Yet the flow of lines does not rest there, but carries one on, over long diagonals and undulating waves, left to the figure of Christ and around the elliptical group.

Among the limitations, which are often overlooked in the present worship of Giotto, is the flat blue background which cuts off space just behind the figures on the left and the hill on the right. This is characteristic of Giotto, and is a surviving medieval trait. It means that the space in which he works is shallow, not genuinely deep as in the ancient Roman *Odyssey* frescoes, or as in Masaccio. Blue as a background has this advantage over gold, however, that it cuts off space less decisively: it recedes quietly, and suggests in an abstract way the infinite depth of the sky. It also serves to render the design of nearby masses more compact, walling them in from the rear. Gold haloes in relief, another medieval survival, further weaken the illusion of depth, by bringing supposedly distant heads forward to the surface of the wall. As in Duccio, Martini and others of the time, there are still groups of figures huddled tightly together (e.g., above the man with hand to chin) with practically no spatial intervals between them. The individual figures are still rigid by comparison with the ancient Roman or with Masaccio; though expressive dramatically, they are frozen into *tableaux vivants*, with little illusion of movement in process. Their voluminous draperies, coming almost to the ground, make them rather block-like, heavy; rarely do they stand on their own feet even as lightly as the two boys lifting the slab in this picture. About color and facial expression one can only surmise, in most cases. Six centuries of damage and repeated restoration have left many successive coats of paint beside the vestiges of Giotto's. The arrangement of different colors into patterns, one may hope, still follows his; but hardly their intrinsic surface quality. Around many of the expressive faces, heavy-handed retouchers have left thick, inflexible, exaggerating lines.

Most of these limitations, it will be noted, are faults chiefly from the standpoint of realistic representation. As pure designs of masses, Giotto's pictures far outrank the Romans' or Masaccio's, and stand among the greatest of all time.

VENICE

Fortunately for the rest of the world, the glorious products of Venetian art in the sixteenth century are scattered to its four corners. Yet the energy of their makers was so prodigious that dozens of small, out-of-the-way churches in Venice are provided with altar-pieces by Bellini, Titian, Tintoretto and their able followers. There has even been a movement in recent years to return some of the paintings from museums to the churches for which they were painted: Titian's *Assumption*, for example, which once more adorns *I Frari*, together with a great *Madonna and Saints* by Giovanni Bellini. One who restricts himself to the *Academy Museum* in Venice will miss several of the finest works.

In addition to those mentioned below, the traveller with a little time to spare will find it worth while to visit *San Giovanni Crisostomo*, for its late and fully developed BEL-LINI *Group of Saints;* the Church (near the School) of *San*

Rocco for its *Christ Bearing the Cross*, attributed to GIOR-
GIONE; *Sta. Maria della Salute* for TINTORETTO's *Marriage at Cana*, and *San Sebastiano* for a number of works by
VERONESE. *The Tempest*, by GIORGIONE, is one of the
most important Venetian works in existence; it is shown at
certain times, in the private *Palazzo Giovanelli*. The *Cà
d'Oro*, another palace famous for its architecture, contains
a rather over-rated group of paintings, of which the best is
MANTEGNA's *St. Sebastian*.

The Academy

TITIAN. THE DEPOSITION. (*Fig. 60; Rm. II, No. 400.*)

This is Titian's last work, unfinished when he died at
ninety-nine. It is not striking at first sight, and one is apt
to pass it by in haste to get to the brilliant Veronese in the
neighboring room. But look long, from a little distance, and
its soft floating outlines will take shape and position; its
dark green shadows will disclose a majestic underlying harmony of sombre colors. It has a quality often found in the
works of an artist's old age: that of extreme breadth, simplification, concentration on a single interest, neglect of
everything irrelevant. That quality appears to some extent
in all great art; but when a man is young, and has not found
himself, he tends to try more different things in the same
work, and to include unnecessary details for no other reason
than that they exist in the model, or in other pictures he
has seen. Titian's late works are extremely specialized,
rigorously pruned down, indifferent to popular taste. But
the enormous range of his genius, compassing in essence
every type of pictorial value known to the history of art,
forbade him to specialize on any one effect repeatedly. His
late works are greatly varied, and astonishingly prophetic
of future tendencies. In the *Crowning with Thorns* (Munich

FIG. 60. THE DEPOSITION
By Titian

and Paris) and the *Virgin Suffering* (Florence, Uffizi 3114) he works in the agitated, light-streaked style of Tintoretto and El Greco. In the *Emperor Charles* at Munich, the *Nymph and Shepherd* at Vienna, and in several of the Madrid works, he anticipates the flattened abbreviations and the new color-schemes of Velazquez.

In this *Deposition* he is unmistakably working, and working with mastery, in the field that Rembrandt later made his own. Avoiding bright color-contrasts, he nevertheless, like Rembrandt, achieves an effect of rich color and luminosity by subtle blends and transitions within a restricted range of dark, unobtrusive tones. There is even a Greco-like quality in its unearthly, phosphorescent inner light, ignoring the natural fall of highlights and shadows. The dull green of the stone blocks is raised step by step in luminosity: to the soft polished sheen of the bottom of the concave niche; to the statues, whose apparent monochrome of light and dark is filled with iridescent blues and yellows beneath the prevailing green; to the weird radiance of the naked body; and finally to the warmer golden lustre of the mosaic-filled upper part of the niche. The red, blue and green of the garments and the warm red-brown flesh of the living figures are rich in tint and texture, but subdued in luminosity, as a setting for the pallid body of Christ.

VITTORE CARPACCIO. THE LEGEND OF ST. URSULA. (*Fig. 61; Rm. XXIII, No. 575.*)

In the guise of an old legend, this series of large canvases portrays the brilliant pageantry of Venetian life at the zenith of its power and luxury. There are broad spacious vistas of canals and harbors, castles and marble palaces, ships and gondolas, flags flying, trumpets blowing, crowds of elegant idlers, pompous arrivals and departures, and ceremonious

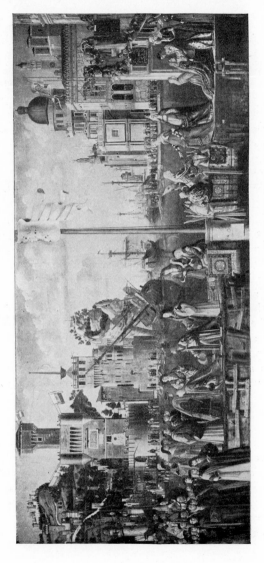

FIG. 61. THE LEGEND OF ST. URSULA

By Carpaccio

processions of nobles and ecclesiastics, magnificent in many-colored velvet, satin, gold and heavy stiff brocade. The sad story of the betrothed couple, ending in the terrific slaughter of Ursula and her eleven thousand virgins, is but a slender connecting thread. The chief interest of the series is direct, in its eye-filling panoply of decorative forms. In the picture illustrated, several incidents of the story are told, with the same characters repeated, and two different places are shown, separated by the flag-pole. But these facts are irrelevant from the standpoint of design: the scene is treated as one broad harbor, filled with one throng of Venetians.

To include so much in one picture without confusion, a high degree of skill at space composition is needed; and in that branch of painting Carpaccio is unexcelled. A good way to measure his ability is to look for a moment in a neighboring room, at Gentile Bellini's *Corpus Christi Procession in the Piazza of St. Mark* (567). That itself is no mean achievement; but it seems monotonous and artificial after looking at Carpaccio. The large area it takes in is box-like, tiresomely regular. The people in it are all too much alike, not only in dress but in posture; they stand bolt upright in long stiff gowns, as vertical as the buildings. Those nearby, in the parade, swing their arms at just the same angle, like soldiers; their heads are on the same level; their coloring is gray and sad. In the center other groups are placed methodically, here, there, and there. They too are stiffly vertical.

Returning to the Carpaccio, what a burst of life and color one feels! This is not through represented action, for the figures are rather quiet; but through the variety of elements in the design. Figures in the row nearest us are kneeling, bending, sitting, reaching, drawing their variegated costumes into sweeping curves and diagonals. A great ship is settled on its side, with its hull making another curve, like the dome on the right, and its long mast cutting across the background in another diagonal. These diagonals are echoed in slanting flag-poles, pennants and stairways. Such repetitions, at various distances from the eye, knit together all parts of space, but there is never too much regularity. Crowds appear far off on different levels; fantastic towers and battlements cut the sky; walls are at different angles; some are flat, some rounded, some rough dull stone and some the tinted green, rose and white marble of Venetian palaces. The expanse of water in the center is empty: a cool green background to rest the eye, and to set off the gorgeous costumes and the oriental rugs to best advantage. In short, space is not only large, and in correct perspective, and filled with objects, each at the distance intended; what is more, space is interestingly filled, with surprising and inventive contrasts of shape and color. And it is unified, made into a self-contained, harmonious world of its own, by constant unobtrusive recurrences of theme.

Color is more brilliantly decorative than in the Bellinis, but also well merged into the general sunlight. In many later Venetian works the pattern of contrasting colors is considerably toned down, to increase the effect of one pervasive golden glow. Here the atmosphere is less rich than in Titian, but a fair share of both values is combined and harmonized.

MARCO BASAITI. THE CALLING OF THE SONS OF ZEBEDEE. (*Fig. 62; Rm. XXV, No. 39.*)

Basaiti is a little-known Venetian, follower of Carpaccio, whose works deserve attention for their distinctive power of deep-space design. The crudeness of his colors and textures, by comparison with other members of his school, is apt to blind one to the skill with which he uses other means.

FIG. 62. THE CALLING OF THE SONS OF ZEBEDEE
By Basaiti

He anticipates the modern cubists in a tendency to divide all objects into distinct planes, and in frequent distortion (notice the boy in the foreground). These planes are triangular, and fit together in a decisive pattern, supported by strong light-and-dark and color-contrasts. The pattern is unified not only by this pervasive rhythm, but by a general converging of planes toward the central figure. Not only the men in middle distance, but the boats below and the far-off hills and walls above, join in this arrangement. The design suffers from a certain lack of harmony between the treatment of figures and of background, in that the latter is given a Venetian mellowness of texture, while the former are carved with a non-realistic, sculptural hardness, full of sudden light transitions, as in Uccello's *Rout of San Romano*. This tends to exaggerate the color-crudeness of the figures. Basaiti was evidently caught between conflicting tendencies of his day, and could not make up his mind to follow out his own distinctive approach with unyielding consistency.

Briefer Mention

TINTORETTO, *Calvary* (Room IX) — unusually symmetrical and tightly woven; saved from confused overcrowding by skillful contrasts of light and color, with a result of compressed, tensely pulsating vibration that heightens the sense of mysterious drama; the color, well preserved, is intermediate between Titian's and Greco's, between rich realism of texture and a fantastic, lurid glow. VERONESE, *Feast at the House of Levi* (Room IX) — colossal in size and in number of figures to be organized. This is done, and the crowd made into one design, by interweaving linear themes in the swaying gestures, and light and color themes in the costumes. The spirit of worldly, irreligious luxury in treating a Biblical theme is typical of Veronese and the late Renaissance. The form as a whole is imposing, dazzling, brilliantly decorative, but without power to move the emotion or imagination very deeply. GIOVANNI BELLINI, *Madonna of the Alberetti* (596) — much restored, and harder in texture than the *Head of Jesus* (87) on another wall; but tenderly human without sentimentality, and pleasant in its bright color-pattern. In the landscape backgrounds of the *Allegories* (595) appears more clearly the deep organic color which Bellini invented, and which formed the basis of Venetian painting. ALVISE VIVARINI, *Madonna and Saints* (607) — stiff, cramped, wooden, sharp-edged figures, basically sculptural; they show the state of Venetian art before Bellini. MANTEGNA, *St. George* (588) — small but concentrated in lustre and grace of line. CANALETTO, *Atrium of a Venetian Palace;* GUARDI, *Islands of San Giorgio Maggiore and Giudecca* (709); LONGHI, *The Apothecary's Shop* (all near the corridor called *Loggia Palladiana*) — these represent the decline of Venetian art in the eighteenth century, with weakened adaptations of the styles of greater men to unimaginative landscape, and to story-telling *genre* scenes.

Church of San Giorgio Maggiore

TINTORETTO. THE LAST SUPPER. (*Fig. 63.*)

With the exception of color, which is better preserved in the Academy *Calvary*, all the outstanding qualities of Tintoretto appear in this strikingly original and complex design. It is characteristic in using intensified streaks of light along limbs and garment-folds, to emphasize the direction of movement, and thus heighten the effect of dramatic action. These twisting, darting gleams of light, flaring out suddenly from deep shadow in the hanging lamp and in the

FIG. 63. THE LAST SUPPER

By Tintoretto

haloes of Christ and the disciples, give the scene an eerie radiance and an air of quivering energy. At the same time they serve to distinguish and organize the picture's many details, silhouetting dark heads against the light, or trans-fixing here and there some white gesturing hand or shoulder against the darkness. Such accents bring out the dramatic and emotional import of each principal element, and its part in the flowing rhythm of movement, while minor details sink into the shadows.

Largely through gradations in light, a distinction is made between the hovering angels and the human bodies below — the former translucent, weightless, insubstantial, vapor-ous forms lit by the flare; the latter lithe but solid, straining muscular limbs. (Such a contrast was later used by El Greco in *The Burial of the Count of Orgaz* at Toledo.) Several of the more sketchy human figures plainly anticipate El Greco's late style in their extreme distortion and simplification by streaks of light — for example, the woman under the lamp in the background, and the two distant servants near the fire-place. Tintoretto, however, never quite loses touch with a basic realism, in drawing bodily proportions, and in expressing the color and texture of objects like the fruit, cloth and glassware.

The composition in space is bizarre and daring, yet suc-cessfully unified. Symmetry is brusquely violated — a step congenial to Tintoretto's uneasy temperament. The table and its row of guests shoot back obliquely, in strange fore-shortening. They diminish in size to an unnatural extent at the farther end, which augments the room's appearance of vast mysterious depth. The figure of Christ, though surprisingly small by comparison with the rest, stands out as a focus of light and color, and as a pivotal center about which the rest of the composition circles. Beginning (let us say) at the lamp in upper left, the movement travels

down and to the right through the servant and disciple at
the near end of the table, on through the cat and three
servants in lower right (their line of heads parallel to the
table) and back overhead through the wings and arms of
the flying angels. This whirling movement is complicated
in two ways: first by minor sidewise whirls and zig-zags, in
the ring of ghostly forms around the lamp, and the swaying,
gesturing limbs of the human figures. Second, it is complicated by swerving backward and forward in the third
dimension: back from the nearby cat and basket to the two
small distant servants at the far end of the room, and forward again along the table.

The result is an amazingly complex, ordered interplay
of dynamic bodies — or rather forces, much less material
than Michelangelo's bodies — in deep space, enriched by
countless variations in the color, light, texture, shape and
posture of the moving parts. The drama of facial expressions, upon which Leonardo relies in his famous treatment
of the same theme at Milan, is almost totally missing. The
gestures, too, are arranged so as to contribute most to the
general motion; not so as to be most expressive emotionally.
Yet the story is conveyed, and its dramatic pace is quickened
by the atmosphere of throbbing, electrical agitation.

School of San Rocco

TINTORETTO. THE ASCENSION. (Fig. 64.)

The restless energy of Tintoretto seldom found complete
expression in pictorial form. Craving always bizarre and
eccentric movements, and one-sided, unstable compositions,
he could never be happy in too tightly, too perfectly in-
tegrated a design. He sometimes tried such designs, but they
are far less typical of his genius than the walls of this building, which he spread with huge agitated figures, straining

FIG. 64. THE ASCENSION
By Tintoretto

to the right or to the left, the top or the bottom of their canvases, with all thought of even balance thrown to the winds. Here he is bound by no formal altar-piece requirements, and he has plenty of canvas to cover with great slashing curves. Whatever color he put on is faded to a dirty brown; but his light and dark are left, impatiently brushing faces, trees and garments into being with long simplified, Greco-like strokes. In their movements we find his nearest approach to a release of pent-up energy; though, by its nature, no one picture could ever be a complete and final expression of it. His cramped *Calvary* at the Academy finds room here to spread out in a larger version over yards of canvas; but it is still basically a symmetrical altar-piece. No single picture comes nearer to expressing the release he sought than this explosive *Ascension*. It bursts into jets of lightning and rising spirals, along the angels' wings and the twisted body of Christ, while the men on the ground below are thrown violently from side to side by its force. This is the Baroque spirit at a moment when it has become fully conscious of itself, freed from irrelevant realism and exulting in the drama of grandiose actions, yet before it has degenerated into empty theatricality.

The Doges' Palace

It is chiefly for architecture and historical memories that this palace can interest the traveller. There are many large and showy paintings here, but few of high quality. The better ones are near the entrance, on the third floor, in the small rooms called the *Anticollegio* and the *Collegio*. The Veronese *Europa*, mentioned below, is here, and some small decorative Tintorettos, especially *Bacchus and Ariadne*. In the Hall of the *Maggior Consiglio* is Tintoretto's huge *Paradise*, utterly disappointing, academic and dead by comparison with his marvellous sketch of the same subject in the Louvre. Elsewhere one sees the fine talents of Veronese and other great artists devoted to covering acres of walls and ceilings with vulgarly overdecorated, though technically dazzling, glorifications of Venetian power and wealth.

PAOLO VERONESE. THE RAPE OF EUROPA. (*Fig. 65.*)

This represents the last great stage of Venetian painting. It carries brilliant decoration almost but not quite to the point of mere ostentatious display. There is still a saving sense of restraint, that restricts the areas of gorgeous texture to a few points of emphasis and thus makes the most of them, not glutting the eye like a stageful of musical comedy costumes. It has lost the austere simplicity, the emphasis on basic structure, the robust vigor, of earlier generations. What associated feelings are expressed are similar to those of eighteenth century French court painting: gay, luxurious enjoyment, a carefree, dancing swirl of pretty faces and shapely arms, fluttering Cupids, roses and satins. The figures have still a basic solidity and strength lacking in Watteau, but the conception is similar to his *The Embarkation for Cythera*, in the Louvre. There is a nearby preparation to depart, then, into the distance, the same figures appear at successive stages of the amorous journey. Watteau has nothing like the dynamic pattern in the foreground, like an intricate sculptural relief, in which the figures of the bull and the maidens, divided into many small masses by deeply indenting shadows, are caught up in a lively, onward-moving rotation. Color and light work in close coöperation with line, dividing the main group into distinct, curving, undulating sections: the bull a soft dull gray-green and brown; three contrasting parts of Europa's robe. Light gives a continuous whirling line along the moving limbs

FIG. 65. THE RAPE OF EUROPA

By Veronese

and folds, and various degrees of light among the women's heads and arms, rising to a climax in Europa's head and shoulder. Color gives its own series of accents, rising from a sombre diffusion of dark blue, crimson and violet in the shadows to a rosy cream with blue shadows in the lighter flesh-tints, and to a climax of richness in the lowest part of Europa's robe, a lustrous gold iridescent with scarlet and orange. Such designs as this later academic painters (Boucher for example) could imitate only as to drawing and surface prettiness; they failed to capture the firm internal organization and substantial texture which raise it to the level of art.

Basilica of St. Mark

BYZANTINE SCHOOL. STORIES OF JESUS. (*Fig. 66; 13th century mosaic, in the nave at the right.*)

The influence of oriental culture, which came by way of Constantinople and through trade in luxuries with the East, was especially strong in medieval Venice. It is evident here in the almost barbaric display of gold and brightly colored stones of which this mosaic is constructed. The fantastic jewelled sprays of flowers are especially lavish in their brilliance. They sparkle in pure contrasting colors with no attempt at shading.

The ancient Roman style of deep, solid, naturalistic painting has been abandoned. Instead, we have a picture almost entirely in one plane, with more distant figures placed above the nearer ones, as in Persian miniatures. This destroys realism, especially in the huddled group of sleeping men, where spatial intervals are ignored. Shadows, too, instead of being placed and graduated naturally, are made into dark heavy strips that outline stiff drapery folds and crevices in the rocks. There is some individuality in the sleeping faces, but much less than in Renaissance painting,

FIG. 66. STORIES OF JESUS
Byzantine School

and the face of Jesus is conventionally impersonal. Postures, too, are cramped and immobile.

All these qualities, which are faults according to Renaissance standards, have a different value as contributing to the kind of decorative effect sought by Byzantine artists. The heavy, narrow shadow-streaks produce a flow of wavy, jerky lines that stream briskly up and down. Since the distant figures, like those of the kneeling Jesus, are as large and distinct as the nearer ones, the upper part of the design is not vague and dull, but a clear, emphatic part of the two-dimensional pattern. There is no attempt to dissolve the wall, and give the illusion that it opens out into space. A wall is expected to be a wall; it should appear as well as be solid everywhere; and that means decorating it with a fairly uniform flatness, throughout.

The three figures of Jesus are arranged as the corners of an inverted triangle, while the rocky peaks point upward. The plants, the garment-folds and crevices are full of smaller angles in all directions. Thus the whole composition is knit together in a zig-zag, vibrating rhythm.

This picture is but a section in a connected series along the wall, and the eye is led from one part to another (here from right to left) through successive episodes of the story, encountering the figure of Jesus in different situations. This way of looking at the parts of a picture in a definite temporal order (somewhat as we look at a moving picture) is common in medieval and early Renaissance art in Europe, and also in the landscape scrolls of China. An interesting element in art was lost when the strict realism of the later Renaissance insisted that a picture contain only what could be seen all at once, from a single point of view.

Throughout the Basilica there are many other excellent mosaics of the Byzantine period: for example, *Building the Tower of Babel* in the atrium (notice the variety of angular movements); and *Events in the Life of John the Baptist* in the baptistery (a fine decorative arrangement of gorgeous costumes, against a background of architectural elements, much distorted in size and perspective to bring them into the pattern).

Other mosaics (upstairs and on the outside) are much later, and are made in imitation of Renaissance painting, with attempts at natural flesh tints, light and shade, gesture and deep space. These attempts are unsuccessful by comparison with good painting, mosaic being too inflexible a medium to secure them easily. At the same time, they lose the decorative appeal of bright, flat, non-realistic color-design, to which mosaic is especially suited. Thus the mosaics of the Middle Ages, like their tapestry and stained glass, are on the whole superior to those of later centuries, because of their greater harmony between form and medium.

OTHER TOWNS IN THE NORTH

Castelfranco, near Padua, has the famous *Madonna with Saints* by GIORGIONE, an altar-piece too hard and symmetrical to express the relaxed, easy suavity of his fully developed style; but ingeniously fitted together of contrasting triangles, light and dark. At *Parma* are the best works of CORREGGIO, especially an *Assumption* and other frescoes in the cathedral.

Ravenna is noted for its BYZANTINE MOSAICS, in the Chapel of Galla Placidia, the Orthodox Baptistery, the Archbishop's Palace, and the churches of San Vitale, Sant' Apollinare Nuovo, and Sant' Apollinare in Classe Fuori. Many of them date from the sixth century A.D. No other town presents so clear and complete a summary of the history of architecture from the fall of the Roman Empire to modern times.

Milan possesses LEONARDO DA VINCI's masterpiece, the *Last Supper,* in the church of Santa Maria delle Grazie. Damaged and restored until little is left of the original surface, its vestiges still sketch an intense drama of contrasting personalities, expressed in face and gesture. The *Brera Museum* contains a famous but immature RAPHAEL *Marriage of the Virgin;* and minor Venetian works, of which a TINTORETTO *Deposition* is the most impressive. In the small *Poldi-Pezzoli Museum* are a pleasantly decorative BOTTICELLI *Madonna* in blue and gold, and a profile, similar to the Veneziano reproduced in Figure 91, whose authorship is still disputed. The *Biblioteca Ambrosiana* is important for illuminated MEDIEVAL manuscripts, and for its Leonardo drawings.

CHAPTER V

AUSTRIA AND GERMANY

THE Renaissance in Germany produced a vigorous school of painting, in which classical elements were successfully blended with the native northern tradition. This school, whose most prominent members were Dürer, Holbein and Cranach, can be seen to best advantage only in the Germanic countries, although there are many fine Holbein portraits in England. In the last few years the so-called German primitives, who lived only a few generations before these prominent men, have been held in increasing esteem. These are still more scarce in foreign museums. To go even farther back: no one can form an adequate notion of Gothic culture, including its remarkable manuscript illuminations, who has not studied its products on German soil. Since the Renaissance, German painting has not yet recovered its former prestige; but the level of critical taste has been high, and museums there contain excellent examples of all foreign schools, including the most radical of modern experiments.

Only the four principal art centers are discussed below; but the traveller with more time to spend can well go on to several others. In *Cologne,* for example, the *Wallraf-Richartz Museum* is rich in early German painters, such as STEPHEN LOCHNER, and the various anonymous artists

known only as " MASTER OF GEORGSLEGENDE," of the
" LYVERSBERG PASSION," of the " LIFE OF MARY," of
the " HOLY KINSHIP," and so on, with reference to their
principal works. The *Colmar Museum* possesses a famous
altar by GRÜNEWALD, which contains the best work of this
powerful artist. *Augsburg, Cassel, Frankfurt, Nuremberg,
Weimar* and *Essen* have good museums — the last-named,
one of contemporary art. From the west of Germany, one
can easily travel on to *Basle,* in Switzerland; from Vienna,
to *Budapest* and *Prague,* all of which have small general
collections of high quality.

VIENNA

The Kunsthistorisches Museum

Though broadly representative, this collection is especially
notable for its Brueghels, for its many Rubens, and for
examples of the Venetian and German schools.

PIETER BRUEGHEL (THE ELDER). THE RETURN OF THE HUNTERS. (*Fig. 67; No. 713.*)

Hundreds of tiny people are scattered over a vast frozen
landscape. We look from a hill-top, over miles of snow, to a
jagged mountain range. We feel a piercing cold in the
blue-green ice below, and in the heavy, dull green sky. It
is heightened by contrast with a tongue of yellow fire at the
left, and with other notes of warm red-brown in the house-
walls there. The black skeletons of trees and bushes, the
black silhouettes of hunting dogs, crows and distant skaters,
and of distant house-walls under snowy roofs, bring out the
dead surrounding whiteness of winter in a mountain village.

All these factors coöperate to produce a vivid sense of

FIG. 67. THE RETURN OF THE HUNTERS
By Brueghel

the "spirit of place" — the concrete, individual reality of this particular scene and occasion. At the same time, they are typical of wintry weather everywhere; they distill the essential spirit of that season; of how things look, and how people and animals feel in the dead of winter. Thus they appeal to a host of deep and vivid associations in the mind of any dweller in a northern climate. This effect had been approached by a few old Flemish painters, notably Pol de Limbourg, but never with this breadth and force, or with this mature command of pictorial means. There is a debt to Venice, perhaps, in the knowledge of how to blend light and color into realistic atmosphere; and Carpaccio had shown a few years earlier how to organize vast spaces, and people them with many little figures. But the materials used, and the total result, are unlike anything imagined in the south. Brueghel's nearest source is Bosch; but there is nothing realistic in that painter's nightmare landscapes filled with imps and monsters.

Surely the birth of modern landscape is here, and not in Claude or Poussin, nearly three quarters of a century later. There is more feeling for nature, as divorced from Greek gods and classical architecture, than in either of these Italianate Frenchmen. Moreover, Brueghel bows to no other landscape painter, from the Sung Chinese to the post-impressionists, in his ability to organize a scene in terms of rhythmic design, and yet maintain that quality of irregular, casual freedom that is vital if the scene is to look genuinely natural.

His design is concealed, but firm and definite. Beside the definite color-themes mentioned — blue-green, yellow and reddish brown — the whole landscape is built out of definite, similar sections fitted together. Strong light-and-dark contrasts bring out a scheme of intersecting diagonals. One of them comes down the nearby slope, from the roof to the

lower right-hand corner. It is answered, unobtrusively, by
another from the lower left, along the bottoms of the trees
and the man's feet, and the edges of the two distant ponds.
This criss-cross is echoed by all the distant roads and roofs,
the spires and mountain peaks. Even the perching crows,
the branches and the bending skaters carry it crisply back
and forth. The lacework of trees, dogs, men and spears
against the snow is as striking as a Japanese print. But it
is not overdone. The background softens to an opal mist
as it nears the horizon, with a realistic sense of aerial
perspective.

JORDAENS. THE BEAN-KING'S FEAST. (*Fig. 68; No. 1087.*)

At this traditional festival, once a year in the Netherlands,
a cake was cut, and whoever found the bean that had been
baked in it was king of the feast. Such a theme of eating,
drinking and carousing, the sheer physical joys (and occasional pains) of uproarious, gluttonous fun, had never been
expressed in a picture with more gusto than in this one,
though it had long been popular in Flemish art. Both the
subject and its expression are such as to offend the more
severe and refined. But the joys of the table are a basic part
of all healthy human life, and the artist who expresses them
vividly will always find congenial souls to carouse with him
in imagination. It is perhaps significant that famine, disease
and war had long ravaged Flanders. A vision such as this
may have been the ideal fulfillment of many dreams.

The pictorial form in which it is expressed is appropriate
and adequate. The warm reds and golds of Rubens fill the
garments and the flushed faces of the drinkers with a ruddy
glow. But the swirling grace of Rubens, his lingering vestige
of classical beauty, has given way to the brutal naturalism of

FIG. 68. THE BEAN-KING'S FEAST

By Jordaens

Caravaggio. The crowded fullness of the composition would be a fault in most pictures; but here the swaying proximity of many stout bodies, the tumbled profusion of jugs and eatables, are all in keeping. The design is unusual: from the dog's leg at the bottom, the lighted strips flare upward and outward like a many branched candle-stick; but with a writhing, flame-like quiver that animates every knotted sinew of the faces and the arms that strain upward in the drinking of the toast.

Abstractly, the rhythm is not dissimilar to Greco's *Pentecost* (the frontispiece) although the subjects are at opposite poles, having only excited exaltation in common. Pictorial, like musical form, expresses in itself only the more abstract, general qualities of emotion.

HANS HOLBEIN (THE YOUNGER). JANE SEYMOUR. (*Fig. 69; Cabinet X, No. 1481.*)

A clear-cut line defines the features with firm, unsentimental clarity. Their pointed sharpness fits into the decorative scheme: a pattern of angles, whose sides are a little bent, into flat rigid curves. These lines, of knife-edge sharpness everywhere, divide the picture into definite sections contrasting in color and texture: red velvet, gray brocade, white lace, flesh, strips of jewelry and a black cap, against a gray-green wall. There is neither richness nor reality to any of these represented textures; all, including the face, have the uniform hardness of painted metal. Their glitter of flat contrasting parts recalls a Byzantine mosaic. Only the face and hands, raised into a low relief, and the slight cast shadows on the robe, are definitely of the Renaissance. This concession to naturalism is just enough to vary and enrich the medieval pattern-basis without discord. As a design, the picture has no subtle, deep relationships to sustain

FIG. 69. JANE SEYMOUR
By Holbein

interest; it is all on the surface, and its first striking decorative
effect soon wears off. There remains a quality of strongly
individualized portraiture. There is not much subtlety in
suggesting character, but there is unusual power to single
out the peculiar contours that make a face distinctive as a
face, and to set down these peculiarities vividly in a few
long, bold, decisive lines.

RUBENS. LANDSCAPE WITH PHILEMON AND BAUCIS. (*Fig. 70; No. 869.*)

One of many outlets for the prolific energy of Rubens
was the painting of landscapes. In this field, as in others,
he was a dominating influence in the Europe of his day.
Like Poussin and Claude, his younger contemporaries, he
derived his inspiration largely from the Venetians. A surviving Renaissance trait, common to all three, is the small,
rather irrelevant group of mythological figures at the right.
His more fundamental debt to Venice, however, is for the
glow of rich, organic colors in the texture of objects and in
their surrounding atmosphere. Although he mixes cooler
and brighter Flemish colors with it, this Italian basis of his
form puts a wide gulf between him and earlier Flemish
landscape painters, such as Patinir and Brueghel. He differs
from Claude and Poussin in inheriting the love of strenuous,
dramatic activity that was Tintoretto's rather than the placid
calm of Giorgione.

Whatever subject he treats, it becomes explosive, tor-
rential, swirling. Nothing in this broad expanse is stable;
everything except the four sheltered figures is caught up in
the grip of raging winds and falling waters; trees are uprooted and torn, and even the rocky hills are twisted into
the same writhing agitation. Flaring colors and flashing
light-and-dark contrasts, in the rainbow and storm-clouds,

FIG. 70. LANDSCAPE WITH PHILEMON AND BAUCIS

By Rubens

contribute to the general excitement. With all this turbulence and fitful lighting, it was hard to maintain definite space relations and a sense of unity. In these regards, the picture is less strong than some of his quieter landscapes (such as the *Chateau de Steen* at London). The right-hand side, especially, is rather dull and confused by comparison with the left.

Melodramatic as it seems today, there is an underlying truth in this landscape, a new grasp of realities in nature, which lifts it above the rank of many pictures more impeccably designed. No one before had expressed so forcefully in paint the wild, disorderly, uncontrolled side of nature, which is quite as real and aesthetically moving as the neatly trimmed parks of Italian painting. Later Dutch painters, especially Jacob van Ruysdael, tried to capture this feeling, but it dwindled to a tame, literal representation of waterfalls and broken trees. Turner was inspired by it, and especially by its dramatic contrasts of tempest and sunshine. It contributed not a little to the Romantic movement in literature and music, with its emphasis on the wildness of nature.

Briefer Mention

RUBENS. Like Munich, this is an excellent place to see the difference between the pictures in which he did most of the work himself, and those left largely to his pupils.* The former are in Saal XIII and Cabinet XIV; the latter in Saal XIV. In his own, even the formal, symmetrical *Ildefonso Altar* (834) is exalted by rich coloring, which contrasts the flaming red-and-gold mists of Titian with the cooler, smoky gray-blues of Veronese, adding many original tones of scarlet and bright blue; the texture is delicately translucent. *The Four Parts of the World* (857) is very

* Cf. p. 217.

uneven, with exaggerated muscles and shadows here and there, and bleak, dead coloring in the stone urn and sky. The *Miracle of St. Ignatius* (865), a school piece, is tediously melodramatic and badly colored throughout. In Saal XV the suave and silky VAN DYCK imitates him with more finished elegance: for example, in *Samson and Delilah* (1043).

There are several inconspicuous little pictures of fine quality. In Cabinet XVIII, TERBORCH's *Portrait of an Old Lady* (1365A) is daringly simplified and impressive in its design of diamond-shaped areas of dull red, black and gold against dark olive; the background plain, the red silks lustrous and finely realistic. In Cabinet XI, JUAN DE FLANDES, a little-known early Fleming who worked in Spain, has two tiny masterpieces: *Christ Bearing the Cross* and *Christ Nailed to the Cross* (631A, 631B) — strongly based on bizarrely distorted zig-zag masses, with deep, delicate, atmospheric tints.

Among the Venetians, TITIAN's *Nymph and Shepherd* (186) is late and highly simplified, into pale, thin mists that suggest some of the eighteenth century French. His *Kurfürst Johann of Saxony* (191) is surprisingly modern in its effect of distortion, to produce an odd design of huge shoulders running up to a small peaked head. The famous GIORGIONE *Three Philosophers* is interesting in its one-sided design, but murky in the shadows. None of the many portraits by VELAZQUEZ has the quality of those at Madrid; and the DÜRER large religious compositions, *Adoration of the Trinity* (1445) and *Martyrdom of Ten Thousand Christians* (1446) are jarring in their lack of relation between the flashy colors and the figures in deep space. Dürer's portrait of *Maximilian I* is plainer but better organized.

The Czernin Collection

This small gallery contains one excellent Vermeer. There is little else of value, although several bad pictures are labelled with great names. A PAUL POTTER *Spring Morning* (187, with cattle and farm-house) is finely drawn and lighted.

VERMEER. THE ARTIST IN HIS STUDIO. (*Fig. 71.*)

The illusion of reality is immediate and surprising. One is suddenly looking into an actual room, full of solid furniture and hangings, in which a painter in Dutch costume sits motionless for an instant to glance at his model. The instant is prolonged, held rigid in eternal calm and silence. The effect is almost hypnotic, and one struggles to escape it by looking at details of the scene. The stiff paper map on the wall, warping and cracking in places; the smooth, demure face of the young model, the heavy curtain nearby, the unpainted wooden easel, the artist's soft brown hair falling to his shoulders — every detail of these defies the longest scrutiny. They are not paint, but real objects in space.

The effect is quite similar to that of Jan Van Eyck's *Arnolfini and his Wife* at London: an initial shock of vivid realism, which continues as one looks more closely, because of the microscopic exactitude of the drawing and the light gradations. Then one feels the more powerful and lasting appeal of design, which raises the picture from a *tour de force* to the level of art. In composition, too, the pictures are basically similar. Each is composed of two motionless persons and a roomful of surrounding objects, lighted by a side window, whose light reveals a pattern of rectangles and curves. As is natural, the Vermeer after more than two

FIG. 71. THE ARTIST IN HIS STUDIO
By Vermeer

centuries of painting is more elaborate, more broadly and massively composed, with all the cramped miniature feeling outgrown. It is more Venetian than Flemish in its method of building up a design of brilliant, rich textures. But the particular materials are quite original.

The principal note is a pure, intense blue, that of some Chinese porcelains, and of the porcelains made at Delft in Vermeer's own day, in imitation of the Chinese. It is peculiarly his own as a factor in painting, and he uses it with great artistry, in countless different shades, blends and substances. Always it is toned to seem an integral part of the object; and in this regard blue has been the stumbling-block of more than one great painter.

One must follow these relations in detail to feel the picture's full charm as a symphony of colors and textures. On the table are cloths of velvet and of silk, in a half-light that shines softly on the folds. They are not a pure blue or yellow, but are mixed with dull, dark green. The curtain is woollen, rough and heavy, with lustreless highlights, flowered in several tones of blue, dark and light, pure and greenish. The floor-tiles are a dark gray-blue and white, with gray-blue streaks. The map is printed in a lighter but duller, grayer blue. In the model's leafy crown, and in the artist's painting of it, the blue is clearer but still has green and even violet admixtures. On the lighted folds of her stiff satin dress, it rises to its highest climax of intensity. Black and red, minor themes, are stated emphatically in the artist's velvet cap and stockings, then echoed in the tip of his supporting rod, and in small spots on the map. They are diffused in a hundred different grays and reddish browns through his other garments, the chair-upholstery, curtain and map-rod. In the model's book a fourth theme of pale yellow is at its purest and brightest; it turns a dark olive in the shadows of her skirts, a dull cream in the plaster mask, a greenish gold in the chandelier, grayish in the easel and brownish in the curtain. It pervades the light generally, giving a cool, clear, un-Venetian atmosphere.

Albertina Museum

A notable collection of drawings, etchings, copperplate engravings, wood-cuts and colored prints. Selected examples are always on display; others are shown by request.

ALBRECHT DÜRER. KNIGHT, DEATH AND DEVIL. (*Fig. 72.*)

Engraving and etching are essentially arts of line. Color is usually omitted, and even though shadows, solid masses, textures and spaces are represented, they are made as a rule by a multiplicity of fine lines, side by side or cross-hatched, close together for shadows or apart to let the paper show through. Dürer's high rank in this medium is much more secure than in painting. His color is often acrid and harsh, and at best adequate in a conventional way. Even in his paintings line is usually the most important factor, as in the *Self-portraits* at Munich and Paris.

Through the engraver's needle his genius for line finds its most adequate medium, and is still a dominating influence in that field. The two examples shown are typical not only of two different phases of his work, but of two different ages in the world's cultural history. Living as he did in early sixteenth century Germany, where the Gothic tradition was still strong, but mingled with Italian Renaissance ideals, he was led to express both. He often combined both elements in the same work, but usually one or the other dominates. In *Knight, Death and Devil* there is Renaissance realism in the solid, accurate modelling and animated move-

FIG. 72. KNIGHT, DEATH AND DEVIL
By Dürer

ment of horse and dog; but it is a minor element in the whole design. The typically Gothic elements are (as to subject and expression) the emphasis on inevitable death, and on grotesque, *macabre* demons. As to form, the picture is Gothic in its intricate linear traceries, like the carvings in a cathedral, or the illuminated initial letters in a medieval manuscript. Line here is developed into a pure music of its own, rather than being subordinated to other elements in form. It curls and flows on endlessly, irregularly, leaving no masses plain, elaborating everything into shaggy, twisting points, producing abstractly that effect of restless, unbounded profusion which the word "Gothic" has come to connote in art.

DÜRER. THE PRODIGAL SON. (*Fig. 37.*)

Here the Gothic element is subordinated. One feels it still in occasional details: the man's fine curling hair, the shaggy bristles of the pigs and distant trees. But now the dominating force is Florentine, and, indirectly, Greek. It appears in the fact that line is mainly devoted to building up a firm, fairly regular architecture of converging solid masses. There is less pure music in the lines themselves: they function chiefly as outlines, to define the edges of houses, man and pigs, and incidentally to enrich the planes with a soft graining of fine parallel threads.

REMBRANDT. EULENSPIEGEL. (*Fig. 74.*)

Where the first Dürer emphasized the music of line, and the second that of masses, this Rembrandt etching emphasizes light. There is no definite linear flow or pattern, and the masses are mostly soft and vague. But such a picture is not necessarily formless, as some modern critics (obsessed

FIG. 73. THE PRODIGAL SON
By Dürer

FIG. 74. EULENSPIEGEL

By Rembrandt

by the current fashion of mass-designs in art) have supposed. The picture is unified aesthetically by the fact that every element coöperates to produce a single, concentrated visual effect. Line and mass are here, but they are not important in themselves. The shapes of things — of boy, girl and animals, brook and hillside, are extremely simplified, and melted almost indistinguishably into one surface, whereon the changing play of lights and shadows can be traced. In painting, Rembrandt produced such effects with brush and pigment; here with a fine needle-point line. But hardly any of the lines are distinct or continuous enough to attract attention in themselves. They wander in fine thread-like tangles, or disappear in thickly cross-hatched areas; now a little closer to produce a delicate shadow; now separating to diffuse the sun. This dominant interest, and the attendant simplifications, relate the picture to modern impressionism. But it is nearer to some of the Chinese and Japanese in its extreme economy of means, and in its entire reliance on subtle gradations in light and dark.

Other Art Collections

The *National Library* has a notable collection of medieval and other manuscripts, containing many fine miniatures and decorative illuminations.

The *Liechtenstein Gallery*, in an imposing palace, is large but on the whole mediocre. Its CHARDIN *genre* scenes on the second floor are among the best of its pictures, but are inferior to those at Paris. Its several large RUBENS are spirited in drawing, especially *Battle and Death*, but drab in color. So second-rate a painter as VAN DYCK stands out favorably with his pretty-girl portrait, *Maria Luisa von Tassis*. There are hundreds of bad Dutch and German pictures upstairs, with here and there a fine one, such as LUCAS

VAN LEYDEN, *Sts. Anthony and Hilary in the Desert,* and
STRIGEL, *Portrait of a Woman.*

Other large but unrewarding collections are in the
Academy of Plastic Arts and the *Graf Harrach Gallery.* In
the Upper Belvedere there are some interesting moderns,
especially in the third and fourth rooms of the *Nineteenth
Century Gallery.* RENOIR has two *Bathers,* and DELA-
CROIX, DAUMIER, COURBET, MONET and PISSARRO are
well represented.

MUNICH

Of all European cities, the Bavarian capital is nearest to
Paris in its general atmosphere of art-production as a vital
public interest. Besides its excellent museums, there are large
temporary exhibitions of contemporary work, in the *Glaspa-
last* and other galleries. They are divided into conservatives
and various shades of radicals, the latter indicated by the
words *Secession* and *Neue Secession.*

The *New Pinakothek,* one of the principal museums, is
still disappointingly given over to academic nineteenth century story-pictures. Cabinet 14 contains a fine CONSTABLE
Wooded Landscape, a COURBET *Still-life* and *Stone Quarry,*
and DAUMIER's *Don Quixote* and *The Drama.*

The Old Pinakothek

Small but high in average quality, and widely representative.

Some of DÜRER's best paintings are here: the *Self-portrait
with Fur Coat,* lustrous in softly shadowed brown and gold,
and tense in its wavering, twining outlines. *The Four Saints,*
his greatest work, is a monumental structure of towering,
statuesque draperies crowned by four massive, rugged heads,

with colors not rich but harmoniously blended. The associations it expresses, intentionally, are the ideals of the German Reformation; sternly spiritual, determinedly independent.

CRANACH the elder is also at his best, not in the popular, whimsical *Venus and Cupid* (this is by the *younger* Lucas Cranach, in imitation of the other's late style) but in the two *Crucifixions* (3819 and 1416). The first of these, especially, with Cardinal Albrecht kneeling, is magnificent and original in design: a dark red robe far to one side, a blood-flecked body, a towering silver tree with lacy, drooping leaves, pale blue and rose gleams against a heavy smoke-gray sky, slashing, intersecting curves of hillside, robe and clouds.

Of the minor Germans, ALTDORFER has a small *Hilly Landscape* (H G 30), done in tiny points of light against dark green and brown, rhythmic but less artificially divided into sections than most early landscape. Its shadowy depths, its intricate feathery, shaggy leaves, twigs and drooping moss, set the tone of German romantic landscape for centuries afterward. STRIGEL's portrait of *Sibylla von Freyberg* (9347) is like a Holbein in its decorative contrast of plain and elaborate surfaces, but more loosely knit, lighter and thinner in color.

GRÜNEWALD. CHRIST MOCKED. (*Fig. 75; Cabinet 4; No. L 2.*)

This is less monumental than the many-winged Isenheimer Altar at Colmar, which ranks Grünewald among the greatest of German painters. But it is a fairly typical piece, combining two different qualities which he often separated. One is a strange, *macabre* imagination: akin to Bosch in its love of weird goblin-shapes; Gothic in its love of grotesque, distorted agonies; Gothic also in its power to

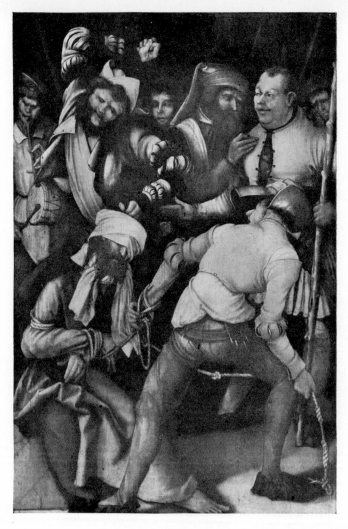

FIG. 75. CHRIST MOCKED
By Grünewald

depict both in a powerful rhythm of twisted line and knotted, lumpish bodies. Another is the command over decorative color, of a blended richness unusual among the Renaissance Germans. The latter he shows also in the large, ornate *Sts. Maurice and Erasmus* (1044); but that is untypical in its bland preoccupation with surface display.

The picture shown has a most original, striking color-pattern of lemon-yellow with gray-blue shadows, white with violet shadows, pale blue, scarlet and deep lustrous violet, finely tinted and yet sharply contrasted. At the same time it has a violent whirl of slashing curved masses, in shallow space, like a carved relief. Grotesque distortions of face and gesture heighten the emotional intensity of the dramatic scene.

PIETER BRUEGHEL (THE ELDER). FOOL'S PARADISE. (*Fig. 76; No. 8940.*)

Good art is not limited to solemn and austere subjects. Too often, it is true, pictures expressing broad slap-stick comedy depend on subject-matter for their appeal, neglecting design. Pieter Brueghel, however, could win the nickname of "Droll Pieter" for his rustic humor, and yet express his jokes in well-organized pictorial form. Neither the joke — soldier, farmer and scholar dreaming of good eatables that get up and walk — nor the form, is especially subtle. But there is something perennially vigorous, healthy and close to the earth, in the rough good spirits of Brueghel's peasant comedies — these sprawling youths, and all his wedding feasts and country sports. And the designs in which his figures are arranged provide an added decorative appeal that is often missing in pictures of like subjects by the Dutch *genre* painters. In addition, they help present the essentials of the story with concentrated force. There are always

FIG. 76. FOOL'S PARADISE

By Brueghel

distinctive formal themes: sometimes everyone and everything is emaciated; sometimes bursting with fatness. Sometimes many tiny figures are seen from a distance, as in the *Return of the Hunters* at Vienna; sometimes large ones close at hand, as in this example. Here there are V-shaped angles (plump legs, tools, roof and tree) contrasting with disc-shaped cakes and table-top. They revolve about the tree like a blissful merry-go-round, slightly reeling and unbalanced; and the empty jug above may be intended as a clue to the reason. The coloring is plain, rich and deep, as befits good food: wine-color, dark reds and yellowish browns against a mossy green hill.

RUBENS. THE RAPE OF THE DAUGHTERS OF LEUCIPPUS. (*Fig. 77; Rm. V, No. 321.*) HÉLÈNE FOURMENT WITH HER CHILD. (*Fig. 78; No. 315.*) OTHERS BY RUBENS AND HIS SCHOOL.

The traveller through Europe's galleries is apt to be amazed, and in time rather wearied, by the enormous number of pictures by Rubens which he encounters everywhere; also by their enormous size and conspicuousness, and their interminable riot of huge, muscular, struggling bodies. Rubens enjoyed an unparalleled vogue throughout Europe in his day, and every palace, to be self-respecting, had to be glorified with some of his grandiose imaginings. Under the conditions of the time, one probably did not have to see him tell the same story so many different times in one summer.

But there is a way to enjoy Rubens; and that is to learn to distinguish what he did himself, and more or less for his own enjoyment, from what he and his pupils did on order, to please the often vulgar taste of princes. It is safe to estimate that nine-tenths of the pictures labelled " Rubens " in the museums of Europe were executed by his school. They

FIG. 77. THE RAPE OF THE DAUGHTERS OF LEUCIPPUS
By Rubens

should be so marked, but that would often be a painful admission. Moreover, they were done from Rubens' sketches, and he may have touched a brush to them here and there, to satisfy his clients.

There is no general way to distinguish one type from the other except through the quality of color. The school pictures everywhere tend to be crudely glaring, a tinselly, superficial scarlet and gold, like a circus wagon; or else drab and dead. His own, especially the later ones, have a richness of texture comparable to the great Venetians. On the whole, too, one is wise to look more carefully at the small, inconspicuous pictures in side rooms, frankly labelled "sketch," than at the huge ostentatious canvases. They are more apt to be entirely by his own hand, and to have a free, spontaneous power that is lacking in the finished pictures made from them. They, and the larger pictures that are more certainly his own, will not disgust the discriminating observer with an over-dose of fleshy exuberance. His love of physical robustness — not fatness, but solid muscle — is there, and his love of sweeping curves, ruddy coloring and strenuous action. They are all related phases of a tremendous physical vitality and love of life that only the puny or ascetic will disapprove. But the artist's sense of restraint keeps them within moderate bounds; and a strong basis of organic light and color prevents the internal weakness that gives to his pupils' works an effect of bombastic pretense. What he thought of the latter, and of some of his noble patrons, is a secret that died with him — but why, in the grandiose *Coronation of Marie de Medici* in the Louvre, does a dog in the foreground turn his back, quite unimpressed, to hunt for a flea?

These general comments might have been made with reference to the Rubens at Paris, Vienna, or any one of several other places. But here at Munich is an excellent place, because of the quantity and variety of its examples, to pursue the problem of distinguishing the sheep from the goats. There are many intermediate breeds: often Rubens is known to have painted some particular part, a capable pupil such as Van Dyck some other, and unknown, inferior hands the rest. (See the official museum catalogue for such known facts.) Examples of pictures in which Rubens did little but the sketch are *Lion Hunt* (602) and *Hippopotamus Hunt* (4797). In *The Rape of the Daughters of Leucippus* there was probably some assistance, but most of the color is of high quality. In *Hélène Fourment with her Child*, in the sketches for the *Medici Series* (92–108), in the *Battle of Amazons* (324) and several others, we can be fairly sure of recognizing Rubens' hand.

The design in the *Daughters of Leucippus* is characteristic in its swirling movement of solid masses, more robust than in Veronese's *Europa* (Fig. 65) and nearer to Michelangelo. The color quality can be appreciated by comparing it with Jordaens' *Satyr and Peasant* (425) and Boel's *Animals and Fruit* (1269). These have black, murky shadows, not only in the backgrounds, but on the figures. They are colorful only in the highlights, and there rather crude, superficial, with over-sudden, disjointed transitions from light to dark. Looking back to the Rubens, one feels at once an iridescent, opal-like scintillation of varied tints and gleams. There are no murky shadows; all are filled with color, as in a late Titian; but the colors are more Veronese-like, lighter and brighter than Titian ordinarily used. Furthermore, the color in the shadows is often quite different in hue from that in the highlights — a method followed by the impressionists in the nineteenth century. Renoir especially, in his late, post-impressionist works, such as the large *Nymphs* recently placed in the Louvre, is indebted to Rubens for his emphatically rotund modelling with brilliant, contrasting color. The essential interest of impressionism is anticipated here by Rubens, in giving objects not only their intrinsic, "local" colors — greenness in a leaf, or redness in an apple — but also subtle tints reflected from nearby colored objects. In the flesh-tints of these women, there is not only a local cream-color, enriched by underpainting of blue veins and surging blood beneath the skin; a red garment is reflected in one place, blue and olive armor and vegetation in others. The hair is never a uniform gold, but is underpainted with brown, olive and violet, deeply lustrous. Even in subordinated parts, this rich luminosity persists — the dark brown chest of the horse is full of deep orange, green and purple undertones, and the glowing sky at the right is suffused with pale watery lemon, rose and gray-blue. Definite contrasts reinforce the main design and its movement: the two women's bodies make a minor pattern in themselves, because of their similar shape and color. Around them is a circling of the darker forms of horses, men and vegetation, brown, gray and green. These are interspersed by streams of warmer color flaming out from the center, in the horseman's orange-red cloak, the crimson cloth on which he lifts the woman, the other woman's flowing pale gold hair and the glistening dark gold satin cloth beneath her.

In the portrait of *Hélène Fourment with her Child* we see the little-known, more delicate and quiet Rubens, not only in the subject and the mood expressed, but in the form. Happily forgotten for a moment is the Rubens of struggling giants, flaming in loud scarlet and gold. The throbbing, swirling rhythm has subsided to a playful, easy back-and-forth of gentle brush-strokes. Every texture has the filmy translucency that appears at times in Goya — thin washes of cool color through which the orange underpainting glows but faintly. They build up a delicate structure: a tilted hat

FIG. 78. HÉLÈNE FOURMENT WITH HER CHILD
By Rubens

with its violet plume, a crumpled soft green velvet jacket, a gauzy skirt of white veil-like chiffon, a purple robe of heavier material, a polished gray granite column, with a vine and twisted orange curtain, a sunny sky and a stool which echoes darkly, under thin crimson and purple streaks, the orange of the curtain. There is no literal copying of materials; everything is given a diaphanous, shimmering texture, full of half-hidden and reflected tints. This is painting in terms of pure color, at its best. Only the figure of the child, with the mother's hands about him, assumes the firm roundness of solid matter, as a point of emphasis. Around are only floating rainbow tints half materialized into hints of silk, hair, feathers, wood and stone. Rubens is here very close to one of the earlier, less sculptural styles of Renoir.

Briefer Mention

BOUTS, *The Taking of Christ* (990); MASTER OF THE PEARL OF BRABANT, *Adoration of the Magi* (H G 76–78) — worthy followers of Van Eyck in combining lustrous color, fine detail and firm basic design. BROUWER, *Fiddling Peasants* (629A) — broad, soft strokes with Rembrandtesque shadows; like Brueghel, he expresses rustic fun in fairly solid patterns; but they are very simple and obvious, and lack color.

TITIAN, *Emperor Charles V* (632); *The Crowning with Thorns* (2272) — distinctive late works; one anticipates Velazquez in flattening subordinate parts, omitting shadows and contrasting thin color-patches; the other is in Tintoretto's agitated, light-streaked style. Unusually good works of POUSSIN, CLAUDE LORRAIN, CHARDIN and BOUCHER are in neighboring rooms.

The New State Gallery

There is one excellent room of French moderns here; the rest are unimportant.

EDOUARD MANET. THE BOAT. (*Fig. 79.*)

In the epoch-making impressionist movement of the 1870's in France, Manet and Claude Monet were leaders. Manet in his early works had revived the Spanish style of painting, that of Velazquez in particular, in long, broad, rough, abbreviated strokes, with a tendency to flatten out the masses least important in the picture. His early paintings are rather dark; but later on, as in this one, he fills these flat strokes with sunlight and color. In places where an especially sparkling effect is wanted, such as the water-reflections at the left, he also uses the impressionist "broken color" technique — small distinct strokes of contrasting color side by side. But he uses it less constantly than Monet, contrasting such places with broad solid areas like the light blue cabin of the boat, and the man's light yellow trousers. These areas are luminous in a way that few other painters have been able to duplicate. It is due not only to skillful blending of tints within each area, but to juxtaposing them with the proper contrasts. They produce the added value of definite color-pattern, often lacking in Monet's soft hazes. Cast shadows are used, but displaced or omitted with great freedom. They are put on where the pattern seems to need a contrasting dark patch, and omitted when it needs a broad light patch. Sometimes they are elongated, to serve as broad, irregular, ribbonlike outlines, and thus accentuate the divisions of the design. A comparison of these points with the Utamaro print (Fig. 15) will reveal the importance of the Japanese influence at this stage

FIG. 79. THE BOAT
By Manet

of Manet's career, mingling with Spanish and impressionist influences.

He builds up a firm basic design of long straight lines and flat curves, emphatically rhythmic, then leaves other parts (such as the woman in the doorway) very sketchy and vague. The right of the artist thus to omit details of nature, if he does not require them in a particular design, was one of the chief doctrines of the impressionists against the academic conservatives of their day. The latter called such pictures as this mere unfinished sketches. But from the artist's point of view, and from that of modern criticism, the picture is finished when he has said what he has to say.

CÉZANNE. STILL LIFE. (*Fig. 80.*)

Whether Cézanne painted a head, a mountain, or a piece of fruit on a table, his tendency was to change it into something more colorful, more plain, massive and rhythmic in shape, than it was in nature. He passed through an early impressionist period of specialized interest in bright surface reflections, and is here attempting a new and difficult problem. This is to combine bright impressionist color with the solidity and clear space relations of the old masters. For the latter qualities, he is obviously indebted to Chardin in this picture. But it differs in being more simplified, less realistic in outline and surface texture, as well as more intense and bright in color.

The shadows are not merely darker shades, grayer and browner, of the same hues employed in the highlights. They are definitely contrasting hues: greens, slate-blues and violets, where the highlights are cream, salmon and red. The paint is laid on in fairly distinct, small areas of different tints, as in pure impressionism. But there is this difference: that they are so arranged as to produce an effect of solid

FIG. 80. STILL LIFE

By Cézanne

modelling, through the tendency of certain colors (especially blue) to recede from the eye, while others (such as red) seem to advance. Still further, the colors are arranged so as to rise from a dull, cool background to a climax of intensity, warmth and richness in a particular spot.

From the standpoint of abstract form, the composition is similar to that of Goya's *Maja Nude* (Fig. 36). In both cases the picture is divided into three main sections: in one, a wall, a draped couch, a nude figure; in the other a wall with chest of drawers, a draped tablecloth with other objects, and a group of apples. In both the three main sections are concentric, the function of the first two being to push forward the third, and lead up to it as a climax of solidity and color-power.

Here the climax is in the apples near the center. They are hard, round balls of flaming red and yellow, blended with the utmost richness, and set off by intense dark green shadows. Around them is a secondary cluster of masses — dishes and table-cloth folds. These are intermediate in accent, both as to color and solidity. They form an irregular scatter of planes at different angles, repeating roughly a triangular and an S-shaped theme. They are less vigorously rounded than the apples, and are colored in duller, cooler tints of gray-blue, yellow and green. The background is lowest in key, and recedes unobtrusively. It consists of a table, a chest of drawers and a bit of wall-paper, which quietly echo the shapes of the objects on the table. S-curves appear in the wall-paper; balls and ellipses in the drawer-pulls and key-holes; angles in the boards of the table. Except for the flowered paper, they are all in broad, dull sheets of rather uniform greenish brown and ochre.

Free irregularities and breaks in symmetry keep the design from being obvious. It flows from part to part with casual ease, yet each part clicks into place with inevitable rhythm. In a precisely analogous way, Cézanne builds up the trees and slopes of a landscape, or the features and garments of a portrait, into an organized design that rises to a climax in some ruddy flesh-tint or iridescent rock.

VINCENT VAN GOGH. VIEW OF ARLES. (*Fig. 81.*)

Van Gogh's early works are heavy, muddy imitations of Millet and Courbet. Later, he learns from the impressionists the secret of broken color, and with it paints landscapes full of natural, sparkling sunlight. Later still, his colors grow even more intensely brilliant and contrasting than those of the impressionists. He leaves out gradual transitions and quiet, neutral areas, laying on pure cobalt blue, chrome yellow, emerald and vermilion side by side in Hals-like strokes which are so coarse the eye cannot blend them (as it can in a purely impressionist painting) into a mild iridescence. They glare, blaze and clash with barbaric exuberance. Such discords are not to be dismissed as bad art: children and primitive peoples, and moderns that have grown used to them, find them pleasantly vigorous and stimulating. The bizarre distortions of shape in Van Gogh's later works are in the same excited spirit. As in an El Greco, everything is made to writhe and zig-zag in nervous agitation. But Greco's motion, like that of Tintoretto and Rubens, was fundamental and powerful; Van Gogh's is sometimes little more than a fantastic surface pattern, or a mere uncontrolled squirming of paint across the canvas.

The landscape shown is fairly late, but with surviving impressionist traits. The writhing, dashing brush-strokes, which were to gain in frenzy till they swept up rocks and houses in one reeling cataract, are here still restrained by some regard for natural outlines. They agitate, but still follow, the trunks and branches of the trees; they leave

FIG. 81. VIEW OF ARLES
By Van Gogh

a fairly natural perspective over fields and blooming orchards to a static group of houses. But the colors are keyed up beyond nature, and separated into large contrasting streaks which refuse to blend into spring sunshine.

DRESDEN

There is a very high average of quality in the small, compact art museum of this pleasant Saxon town. Few bad pictures clutter its walls, and there is every facility for finding and enjoying the best ones.

The picture which the crowds flock to see is the *Sistine Madonna* of RAPHAEL. There is a liberal flavoring of sweetness in the faces and attitudes of the two saints and the cherubs. But in the Madonna and Child themselves, there is much less than in his earlier works. From the standpoint of design the picture's distinctive feature is its contrast of the dark figures, green and gold, against a cloudy white background. This is striking, but offers no long-continued interest; at bottom, the picture is still the conventional, oversymmetrical altar-piece. The coloring of the robes and faces achieves a rich texture attained by Raphael only in his last few pictures; it is unsurpassed among the Florentines, but common enough among the Venetians from Giovanni Bellini on. The movement of line from figure to figure is continuous and forceful. By substituting an irregular spiral whirl for the usual balance of static, vertical forms, it partially compensates for the tedious regularity and shallowness of the composition as a whole.

GIORGIONE. THE SLEEPING VENUS. (*Fig. 82; Rm. G.*)

The *Sleeping Venus* of Giorgione is one of the great works whose power must be traced to its perfect inner harmony, rather than to any particular distinctive feature. It represents a moment of balance and merging between several different tendencies, all of which are isolated, carried to extremes, and made to clash irreconcilably, in other works of art. For example, it includes some of the typical qualities of Greek sculpture: the idealized, regular face and long, graceful bodily contours. But the face and body are not made regular to the point of becoming abstract and inhuman; nor are they hard and stone-like, or sharply linear (as in Botticelli and Ingres, for example). They are infused with warm, blended tints which add reality and decorative richness, and these are contrasted with the textures of crimson and silver-gray draperies, and soft green landscape. But the richness and contrast of textures are not raised, as in later Venetian work, to be ends in themselves. There is rhythmic repetition of lines and planes in the slopes of the hills, the folds of cloth and the contours of the body; but these are not emphasized to the point of artificial pattern. There is illusion of reality in the landscape, and in the figure, but not photographically detailed. Space is deep, and adequately filled to sustain interest, but not enough to require fatiguing effort in taking it all in at once. Deep human interests are appealed to: the sexual interest of a beautiful body, and of an attitude of modest concealment; the charm of a broad, well-kept, rolling landscape, drawing the eye over long flights that expand one's imaginary reach; the associations of old houses, and of feathery trees reaching into the air; the rich literary associations of Greek mythology; the lulling, quieting air of brooding peace, safety and serenity, expressed in both figure and landscape. But none of these is obtrusively accented, and none conflicts with any other. The producing of all these effects with comparatively few parts, few details, few contrasting themes, accounts for the picture's net effect of simplicity. Though

FIG. 82. THE SLEEPING VENUS

By Giorgione

Titian is thought to have completed the landscape, there is little of his more masculine, rugged vigor in it, or of his tendency to elaboration; less even than in the Paris *Concert Champêtre*. This and its unruffled air of gentle tranquillity make it the most typically Giorgionesque of all the pictures attributed to Giorgione.

Briefer Mention

VERMEER, *At the Courtesan's* (1335) — most unusual for this painter, in its big, spread-out, ostentatious pattern, its emphasis on facial expression and gesture, and its spirit of ribald fun. There is good color in the modelling of the girl's face and cap, but the rest of the picture has deteriorated, or has been painted by some inferior hand. *Girl Reading a Letter* (1336) is a more typical and harmonious Vermeer. REMBRANDT's *Man with Pearl-trimmed Hat* (1570) is one of his best late portrait heads, magically lighted as usual, and poignantly expressive in its contrast of fine raiment with despairing, withered old age. RUBENS, *Wild Boar Hunt* (962) — worked with exceptional fineness of detail for him, but with no sacrifice of dynamic energy, shock and tension in its whirlpool of slim, wiry dogs and twisted fallen branches; the forest is an exquisite tapestry of tree-forms. JACOB VAN RUYSDAEL, *The Jewish Cemetery* (1502) — the essential spirit of the romantic movement is in this landscape, a century ahead of its time: in subject, ruined towers, lonely graves, gnarled trees, rushing water and an approaching storm; in form, melodramatic contrasts of gloom and eerie light, in dashing, irregular streaks. VAN EYCK, HOLBEIN, CANALETTO, POUSSIN, LANCRET AND WATTEAU are well represented.

Modern Section

In another part of the museum is a small collection of late nineteenth century French and German pictures. In the sentimental BÖCKLIN, one can see the last weak flutter of the romantic movement. There are typical works of PUVIS DE CHAVANNES (*Fisherman's Family*, 2523); MONET (*The Seine near Lavacourt*, 2525A); VAN GOGH (*Pears*, 2593); TOULOUSE-LAUTREC (*Studio Scene*, 2603) and GAUGUIN (*Women of Tahiti*, 2610).

COURBET. THE STONE-BREAKERS. (*Fig. 83; No. 2522*.)

This was an epoch-making picture when first exhibited, and it sums up, more clearly than his larger pictures in the Louvre, the distinctive features of Courbet's art. Classified under the vague word "naturalism," it stood for a conscious reaction away from both Ingres and Delacroix; away from two different styles, both artificial and conventional, in Courbet's opinion. One was that of cold, precise, linear classicism; the other that of romanticism, with its flamboyant swirls, its flaming colors and its theatrically passionate subject-matter. Against both of these traditions Courbet championed another: that of representing life and nature as they are, unidealized, in all their crude, simple vigor.

For a subject, he chooses in this picture humble workmen; he gives them no sculptural grace and no exotic allurements; no finely balanced, neatly organized design. All such qualities, praised in other pictures, would conflict with that of truthful representation, which he most desires.

The tendency thus revived was beneficial, in that it led painters back to more direct observation of nature, and a quest for new, unconventional designs. It was not a new

FIG. 83. THE STONE-BREAKERS
By Courbet

movement, for in their own time several Italian, Dutch and Spanish painters, as well as Louis Le Nain, Chardin and Millet in France, had stood for reactions "back to nature." Such movements are periodic, and their ultimate effect is usually to introduce some new convention, some new artificial way of looking at nature. For the artist must select from nature, and reassemble what he selects into some sort of new, ideal form.

In this picture, and in Courbet's art in general, the most important element is not mere truthfulness in representing nature, but the distinctive ways in which he transformed what he saw. One of these was to intensify the surface richness of the most ordinary materials. There is a silvery, mossy sheen to these rocks, a deep, juicy coolness to the grass, and a dark lustre of creamy brown and gold to these ragged garments, that is not unnatural, but more intense than anything ordinary eyes could see. They combine to make a consistent color-harmony, that implies much altering and eliminating on the part of the painter: the dinner-pail must be made more silvery, the bread a richer brown, and the straw a more glistening yellow. And the drawing would not satisfy so well if it did not represent selected attitudes of strain and weary work, more expressive than any casual photograph, and more linked together by hidden repetitions of linear theme. In other words, a new artificial form is created, of fresh, limpid coloring and brusque, irregular, heavy lines.

BERLIN

The Kaiser Friedrich Museum

The picture-gallery is on the upper floor, in a line of rooms around the exterior. Turning right at the head of the stairs, one begins with the early Italian schools; left, with the Flemish, German and Dutch. The Venetian and Spanish are at the far end, reached by either turning.

Since the German and Early Flemish rooms are the most distinctive, it is well to begin there. The Rembrandt room, a little farther, deserves perhaps the longest visit of all; it contains no important large work, but excellent smaller ones in large variety.

The HOLBEIN portrait of *The Merchant George Gisze* (586, in Cabinet 67) is one of the most celebrated works in the collection. It provides an interesting problem for critical appraisal. Like his *Ambassadors* at London, it involves the arrangement of objects at different distances in shallow space, whereas the *Jane Seymour* at Vienna (Fig. 69) is intentionally almost flat. A multitude of small utensils and papers is drawn with minute exactness in accurate perspective. The first impression is of strikingly clear space relations, and also of the quaint, antiquarian associations of all these relics of a bygone age of commerce. Further scrutiny discloses that the objects are inter-related by recurrent themes of shape, color, lightness and darkness, into a decorative pattern which serves as a setting for a clear-cut, handsome face. At the same time it fails to produce that sense of perfect merging into a unified whole which Van Eyck and Vermeer attain in similar compositions, through finer gradations of light and color, and through selective emphasis. The final effect is somewhat edgy, through over-sharp, uniform linear contours; diffuse, through lack of proper accent and subordination, and disunited, through the failure of many parts (especially the glistening red sleeve) to blend continuously with their surroundings.

The several DÜRER portraits, especially *Hieronymus Holzschuher*, are modelled with vigorous, direct naturalism, but are not outstandingly important.

FIG. 84. PORTRAIT OF A YOUNG GIRL
By Petrus Cristus

PETRUS CRISTUS. PORTRAIT OF A YOUNG GIRL. (*Fig. 84; Rm. 70, No. 532.*)

The miniature perfection of early Flemish painting is present in the smooth, enamel-like modelling of the face, and in the tiny details of the necklace and hat-band, studded with small lustrous pearls. But it is not carried too far, into undiscriminating, crowded, microscopic copying of the model. The detailed, highly finished parts are brought out by plainer, flatter, duller areas into strong selective emphasis. There is a fair amount of realistic portraiture: the adolescent face is concretely individualized with a few fine, sensitive strokes in mouth and eyes.

But all of these elements are subordinated to decorative pattern. The clear-cut outlines are well related through repetition: horizontal in the wainscoting, mouth and bodice; slanting in the tall hat and the wide V-neck of fur; semi-circular in necklace and hat-band; a series of small, pointed curves in the chin, nose, ear and the black loop on the forehead. Definite shades of light and dark, flat and rounded areas, are all sharply contrasted in a manner that anticipates Holbein, but with more selective emphasis. The colors and surfaces anticipate Vermeer in their light, cool, fragile daintiness. They are less realistic in texture, less subtly varied in lighting, but similar in decorative appeal and in the particular tints used. These are an intense blue dress, and skin of cream and pale rose with delicate olive shadows, against a plain dark gray-green wall.

LUCAS CRANACH (THE ELDER). APOLLO AND DIANA. (*Fig. 85; Cabinet 65.*)

Like Mantegna's, Cranach's later works show the mellowing influence of Renaissance paganism. In both cases,

FIG. 85. APOLLO AND DIANA
By Cranach

the change is not wholly for the better. Agonizing Crucifixions (like the two at Munich), done in intricate Gothic
line-patterns or in strong plain colors, give way to pert, mis-
chievous little Venuses, naughtily naked in a velvet hat or a
string of beads. As representation, the latter may be more
amusing; but the designs in general grow weaker. The
coloring becomes hard and drab; the figures are brittle imitations of sculpture; the strong fine line gives way to a
facile decorative grace reminiscent of Botticelli's, but often
monotonous and formalized.

The picture reproduced here is a fairly well-balanced
mean between the two extremes. As color it is completely
dead, but its line is still alive, to weave the forms of girl and
stag, man and bow, into a delightful melody of intertwining
curves. The fresh, unsymmetrical pattern they describe, of a
large triangle on its side, is echoed in the background masses.
To the figures' sculptural clarity, they contrast the soft
feathery depths of a German primitive landscape, like those
of Altdorfer. The faces and bodies are not Italianate, but
realistically German in a naïve, dainty way, much less rugged
than those of Dürer.

PATINIR. REST ON THE FLIGHT TO EGYPT. (*Fig. 86;
Rm. 69, No. 608.*)

In making the landscape interest dominant, with human
figures small and subordinate, Patinir stands out from his
early 16th century contemporaries, and anticipates Brueghel
and Claude Lorrain. But his treatment of landscape is
primitive in its unnatural clarity of detail, such as nearby
leaves and far-off, tiny people, undimmed by intervening
atmosphere. Patinir is primitive also in his unnaturally
sudden color transitions. He divides the landscape into sharply
distinct areas of blue and of green, against which the woman's

FIG. 86. REST ON THE FLIGHT TO EGYPT

By Patinir

dress, divided into rose, blue, green and white areas, stands out with equal distinctness. Most unnatural of all is the sharp, highly rhythmic outline that weaves these color-patches and all the myriad small details into a tightly unified pattern. Every line repeats with variation some one of several distinct themes. The winding, zig-zag roads and rivers state the principal theme, and it is carried on with stiff angularity by the limbs and drapery-folds of mother and child. It is softened a little by the winding rows of trees that follow it into the distance with round little balls of stiff jewelled foliage; and it rises jagged and rough in the tree-trunks and the wandering lines of rocky crag. Most of the little houses are pointed, like the angles of the road, but some are rounded like the straw hamper.

Such intricate, detailed repetitions of linear theme produce one kind of value in landscape, that of definite pattern. But they destroy another: the quality of free, relaxed informality which delights us in nature itself. Thus in Patinir landscape is more artificial and lifeless than it is in Pol de Limbourg, his Flemish predecessor, or in many later men who concealed and softened their basically rhythmic designs with free irregularities of detail.

FRANS HALS. HILLE BOBBE, THE WITCH OF HAARLEM. (*Fig. 87; Cabinet 59, No. 801C.*)

Rough, dashing, bristling brush-strokes, thick with paint, sketch the portrait tersely and vigorously. The style is typical of Hals' mature work, and unusually appropriate to this subject — a wild, eccentric character, slightly mad and excited with boisterous tavern mirth. It has more of his distinctive brusque vitality than many of his larger, more carefully studied compositions. There is little color: the dull grays and leathery browns do not heighten the picture's

FIG. 87. HILLE BOBBE, THE WITCH OF HAARLEM
By Hals

vivacity, as do the reds and whites in his *Bohemian Girl* in Paris. But Hals is never remarkable as a colorist. There is little pattern, aside from the simple, obvious diagonal of tankard, face and bird, answered by a few opposite diagonals in the head and skirt. The spirit is one of conscious reaction from the precise designs and refinements of the Italian Renaissance, toward a lusty naturalism that revels in freedom, crudeness and irregular forms. It is at the opposite extreme, too, from the early Dutch and Flemish, with their fine, smooth miniature detail. But the picture is not to be called chaotic or formless, for its parts are harmonized by a single consistent spirit and rhythm of brush-strokes. It is highly selective and simplified, choosing only the few most expressive details of the model's appearance, and putting them down with a highly personal, contagious gusto.

REMBRANDT. THE MAN WITH THE GOLD HELMET. (*Fig. 88; Rm. 61, No. 811A.*)

As usual in a Rembrandt portrait, this is a combination of keen psychological analysis with a subtle, powerful music of lights and shadows. His faces are always full of meaning and of character, strongly individualized through emphasis on a few distinctive contours. They are never bland, impersonal, regular masks, but bear the marks of experience, thought and feeling, which tempt us to wonder what reserves of personality lie behind them. In this psychological interest Rembrandt is akin to Leonardo da Vinci, and also in his reliance upon soft, mysterious shadows as the basis of his form. There is little range or brilliance of color in either. But Rembrandt had profited by sixteenth century Venetian painting, and knew how to blend his colors with light in a way that Leonardo did not, and so to make the most of what he used. In his own works (there are many falsely attributed

FIG. 88. THE MAN WITH THE GOLD HELMET
By Rembrandt

to him) the shadows are never drab and dead, the modelling never hard and sculptural, the transitions from dark to light never flashily theatrical — all faults common in Leonardo. Nor does he rely on a beautiful or interesting face to cover up lack of pictorial form.

As suggested above, his use of light is a kind of music, that can be enjoyed for its rising and falling play over various surfaces, without thought of what it represents. Here there are three contrasted keys of light and shade: first the glittering, strongly lit helmet; second the face in a dull half-light; third the shadowy plumes above and the shoulders below, almost lost in darkness. The same colors appear throughout: a dark reddish brown, gray-green and gold. In the lowest key they are spread in dull vague films, the gray almost obscuring the red. In the face they separate a little to form a gray mustache and shadows, brown weathered skin and dull yellow highlights. The face is stern, rugged, worn, but with a hint of kindly softening in the lines about the eyes. It is the climax of the picture's expressive interest. Yet the face is not the most emphasized part, as a more obvious " character-study " would have made it. In intensity of light, the picture rises to a yet higher climax in the helmet, which, though still dark, is brilliant by contrast with the rest. It is in no glare of sun, but in the indoor yellow gleam of some torch or candle, which flickers on the ridged embossing of the surface. The embossing is represented in a literal way unusual in Rembrandt, and in good painting generally — by actual ridges of paint in *impasto*. But here it does not seem to break away from the rest of the picture, but only to heighten the decorative contrast between the rich, ornamental surface of the helmet and the waxy, smooth, dull face below.

TITIAN. VENUS WITH THE ORGAN-PLAYER. (*Fig. 89;*
Rm. 47.)

This is not one of Titian's greatest pictures, but it represents a mature stage of his development, and it is in an
excellent state of preservation. Such cleaning and restoring as
it has had, have been skillfully done. That cannot be said
for many of his more famous works, which have been
crudely retouched in years past (though the fact is not usually
advertised) or left under centuries of dirt and thickened
varnish. From such undoubted masterpieces as the *Entombment* or the *Supper at Emmaus*, in the Louvre, one gets a
false idea of Venetian color as being uniformly tinged with
a dark golden brown. In Germany and Austria the technique of cleaning and restoring has been well developed —
it is a combination of chemical science with sensitive, modest
craftsmanship. There Venetian and other old masters come
out from behind their films of amber to shine again in fresh,
pure daylight hues.

The picture is one of a series of similar Venuses which
Titian made to order for various patrons, who, it is said,
were allowed to appear as the admiring organ-player. It
has some of the ear-marks of a made-to-order work: a lack
of life and spontaneity in the drawing. There is something
a little forced, as of a conscious theoretical problem, in the
effort to unify two such different elements as are in the
right and left halves of the picture. But Titian is never a
hack-worker; and if it lacks the supreme touch of genius,
it is a work full of interest from the standpoint of design.

Based on Giorgione's *Sleeping Venus* at Dresden (Fig.
82), like a host of later reclining nudes, it is characteristic
of Titian and the later Renaissance in the way it elabo-
rates that simple Grecian theme with a profusion of added
elements. The organ and its player, the dog, cupid, and

FIG. 89. VENUS WITH THE ORGAN-PLAYER

By Titian

overhanging curtain, are all new, and each is the means of complicating the form with some different color and texture. It loses in unity and concentrated force as compared with the Giorgione, but it gains a profusion of decorative materials for the eye to feed upon. We need not stop to dwell upon the careful interweaving of shapes: the repeated angles in the organ, the bearded profile, the hanging curtain, the mountain peak, and so on. Such effects were not distinctive with Titian. Nor was it original with him to construct a pattern of contrasting color-areas, or an atmosphere of blended tints.

But this picture was and still is remarkable as a design of realistic textures, repeated, varied and contrasted with each other. This is the type of design which Veronese, Velazquez, Vermeer and Chardin were later to develop in many different ways, but they added nothing to the basic form presented here. Each part not only has a definite shape, color and degree of lightness, but a distinctive surface consistency. For example, the cold, steely, gray-blue of the organ-pipes, and their hard, rigid, glossy smoothness, serve to bring out by contrast the warm, rosy skin and the soft, yielding roundness of the body. The little hairy dog, the glistening satin pillow and pearls, the wisp of veiling, the cloudy sky and the highlights on the organ — all these are varied tints and textures of the same basic color, white. There is gold in the hair of Venus and Cupid, in her jewelry, and in the hose of the organist. His jacket, the red coverlet and curtain, are all shades of deep purplish crimson, varied as to the lustre on their folds, and as to the amount of brown in them. In the flesh-tints of the Venus, all these colors are blended in lighter shades and in a more delicate, rich tinting. Not only the reds and whites are there, but even the blues and olive greens, in soft shadows and in veins beneath the surface of the skin. (In the nudes of Rubens, this color-richness was still further developed.) It is appropriate, in view of such an interest in textures, that the body is less smooth, slim and firm than in the Giorgione, or than in Titian's younger *Reclining Venus* in the Uffizi. The maturer, softly undulating planes afford more opportunity for the play of different tints and shadows.

CORREGGIO. LEDA AND THE SWAN. (*Fig. 90; Rm. 45.*)

Correggio is one of those painters who rely for a large part of their appeal on exaggerated smiles and languidly graceful gestures. His pictures usually present a hackneyed pattern, made flashily obvious by a pronounced light-and-shade contrast, based on the style of Leonardo da Vinci. This is the celebrated "chiaroscuro," for which he has been given excessive praise. In color, he emphasizes light pinks and blues, of some decorative charm but rarely well organized with other elements. Like many other inferior painters, he outdoes himself at rare moments, and produces a picture of some substance and originality. The *Leda* is somewhat less characteristic than his *Danaë* in the Borghese at Rome, since it makes less extreme use of chiaroscuro. With more moderate, less theatrical light emphasis, he brings out here an equally original and effective design. It is formed by the long, slender shapes of girls, cupids and swans, trunks and branches of trees, which converge and circle toward the face of Leda, bending and waving in a gentle, floating rhythm. His light pinks and blues are here, in the two figures to the right of Leda, but they are better merged than usual in a thin, delicate version of Venetian atmosphere. His pretty smiles are here, but not exaggerated, and not relied on at the expense of design. The result is none too strong, but it is light decoration of a high order. It illustrates how traits that are offensive when overdone in isolation

FIG. 90. LEDA AND THE SWAN
By Correggio

may be pleasing when incorporated in a fairly well-balanced form.

DOMENICO VENEZIANO. PORTRAIT OF A GIRL. (*Fig. 91; Cabinet 30, No. 1614.*)

It is interesting to compare this picture with the Renaissance coins and medals in adjoining rooms, for here the charm of the medal-maker's art is transposed to painting. It is essentially a bas-relief, a finely engraved cameo, in long pure lines, firm and sure, yet sensitive to the contours of the delicate profile. The lines are insistently rhythmic: the curves of the sleeves and bodice repeat those of the head; and in the hair and cap they intertwine again. The color is all on the surface, but is brightly decorative, and in keeping with the hard, flat outlines. Against an intense, dry, light blue, like that of Piero's frescoes, the pale cream and gold of the head is defined with unforgettable clarity; and the ornate brocade of scarlet and gold below relieves the severity of the upper half.

Briefer Mention

TERBORCH, *The Concert* (791G); VERMEER, *Lady and Gentleman Drinking Wine* (912C) — these have the soft lustrous texture, the well-unified design, the continuous, harmonious color-atmosphere, that are lacking in Holbein's *Gisze*. The other works by Vermeer and De Hooch in the same room (57) are inferior. SIGNORELLI, *Pan and his Attendants* (79A) — an example of the typical Florentine form, design through rhythmic arrangement of statuesque bodies in space, carried out with a too obvious regularity which makes it tiresomely academic. The LIPPI *Madonna Adoring the Child* (69), similar to one in the Uffizi, is more original and imaginative in its decorative

FIG. 91. PORTRAIT OF A GIRL
By Domenico Veneziano

scheme: the light blue, enamel-like drapery against a tapestry of rocks and trees, flattened into a soft, dull, contrasting background. KONRAT WITZ, *Christ on the Cross* — an unusually powerful color-design for the early fifteenth century.

Other Picture-galleries

The *Crown Prince's Palace* has been transformed into a museum of modern art, known as the *New Section of the National Gallery.* Besides changing exhibitions, it has several excellent French impressionist and post-impressionist pictures. RENOIR's *Blooming Chestnut Trees* (1007), of his impressionist period, is a soft cloud of floating, spring-like pinks and pale greens. MANET's *In the Winter Garden* (693) shows his flattened, Spanish style before it had attained full luminosity of color. The CÉZANNE *Landscape* (743) and *Still-life* (887, 888) are fairly typical of his stronger, post-impressionist style. Among the recent German works often shown are distinctive water-colors by KLEE and expressionist oil paintings by MARC and KOKOSCHKA.

The *Old Section of the National Gallery,* in a large building by itself, has little to offer but hundreds of academic story-pictures of the nineteenth century, weak, stereotyped imitations of David, Ingres, Delacroix and other leaders of the time. Some second-rate pictures by Delacroix himself, by Goya, Constable, Daumier and Courbet, stand out favorably by contrast.

In the *Museum for Ethnology* (*Völkerkunde*), paintings and other antiquities from Central Asia, India, China and Japan are being assembled.

CHAPTER VI

BELGIUM AND HOLLAND

A TRIP through the small museums of the Low Countries
is primarily for those who have formed a taste for Dutch and
Flemish painting elsewhere. Their exhibits are restricted
rather narrowly to these local schools, which can be seen
to advantage without going to Belgium and Holland. But
for anyone who has felt the peculiar charm of northern
painting, the occasional Van Eyck or Bouts which he has
seen elsewhere, gleaming out like a small jewel amid wastes
of arid canvas, is but an inducement to seek more of the
kind. The popularity of Dutch landscape, *genre* scenes and
portraiture is more widespread, and the knowledge that
good Vermeers and Rembrandts are in Holland draws a
steady stream of pilgrims there. The examples mentioned
below represent the leading members of both these schools.

ANTWERP

ROGER VAN DER WEYDEN. THE SEVEN SACRAMENTS.
(*Central panel; Fig. 92.*)

The knife-edged linear drawing is impressive with its
fine precision, but in time a little tedious for its uniform edgi-
ness. It engraves a meticulous pattern of tiny angular

FIG. 92. THE SEVEN SACRAMENTS
By Roger van der Weyden

drapery-folds, of stiffly gesturing limbs and intricate Gothic carving, against the grandly tall, unbroken, upward-sweeping outlines of the cross, the columns and the vaulting. The colors likewise form a studied pattern of contrasts: of intense, velvety reds and blues against the pale, cool gray-green stone. At rhythmic intervals in space little distant figures, columns and an altar stand frozen in a strange world of unnatural clarity, their details too microscopically distinct, their tiny highlights and shadows too exactly and regularly placed, to be realistic. It is a vision that fascinates, in a dream-like way. But it suffers from a lack of selection and emphasis, and of the softening, uniting touch of diffused and reflected light — all qualities not lacking in Roger's older and greater contemporary, Van Eyck. The faces are exquisite cameos, yet a little affected and theatrical in their grief. As both decoration and representation, the picture tends toward hard, academic formalism, but it commands respect for the technical skill with which it carries out a large, complex design.

Briefer Mention

Others in the Art Museum: PIETER BRUEGHEL (or BREUGHEL), *Adoration of the Magi* — there are three Pieter Brueghels, the elder, the younger and the third, in addition to a Jan Brueghel. The elder is the great one; the others of the same name imitate him rather weakly, but the picture-labels often fail to indicate which is which. The one mentioned may be by the elder, but it is inferior to those at Vienna. Another of the same sort is *Visit to the Farm* (645). GERARD DAVID, *Rest on the Flight to Egypt* — a pleasant, cool, green landscape, with figures inclined to softness and conventionality. MASSYS (QUENTIN), Trip-tych: *The Entombment and the Martyrdoms of Sts. John the Baptist and John the Evangelist* — important transitional works showing the influence of Italian coloring and modelling on the Flemish school; strong, unconventional designs of large, angular color-planes.

In the *Cathedral* is the famous *Descent from the Cross* by RUBENS; its color has faded until it no longer represents him at his best.

BRUSSELS

DIERIC BOUTS. THE JUSTICE OF OTTO: TORMENT OF THE INNOCENT. (*Fig. 93.*)

This large panel and its companion, *The Ordeal by Fire*, were the crowning achievements of Bouts' career, unfinished at his death. Their supposed completion by his son, or their long exposure in the Town Hall at Louvain, may explain why their coloring is more hard and lustreless than in some of his smaller pictures — those at Munich, for example. But in other respects they are among the most powerful of early Flemish works. Their boldness and originality can best be felt by contrasting them with the dead symmetry, the few stereotyped patterns, the trivial miniature detail, of most of the contemporary paintings nearby.

The firm, stately dignity of these figures, and the rugged plainness and realism of their faces, recall Piero della Francesca. But their rhythm is more severe and adamantine. They are tall, thin, straight and rigid, bending only in angles; yet somehow not cramped in gesture. Their firmness is internal, massive, not the superficial tightness of line that binds academic medieval art. Nor are they cramped in space: they stand detached, independent, a succession of slender columns about the flint-like headsman. They march out of space in a series of groups, from a background of

FIG. 93. THE JUSTICE OF OTTO
By Dieric Bouts

towers and battlements no more straight and unyielding
than they. In a series of diagonal steps of hammer-like de-
cision, they move over ground that tilts downward to place
them on successive levels. The foremost stand at the sides,
two inexorable symbols of medieval justice.

HANS MEMLING — THE MARTYRDOM OF ST. SEBAS-TIAN. (*Fig. 94.*)

With the beginnings of Italian influence, the sharp edgi-
ness of Flemish art is a little mellowed, with softer tints and
contours. The frozen gestures and garment-folds relax, and
gentler shadows sweep over broader surfaces, wiping out
a host of small details, though many still remain. The agonized facial expressions, a heritage from the Middle Ages,
give way to blander, happier ones — sometimes, as here, less
forceful and less appropriate to the subject. But the deep,
cool color and smooth oily surfaces of Jan Van Eyck remain,
glowing with a dark lustre of ruby velvet against green
vegetation, and blue sea, and fading to soft browns in fur,
wood and landscape. The result is a peculiar kind of richness, unattainable in Florentine tempera or fresco, yet without the warm melting texture of Venetian oils. There remain also, of the earlier Flemish form, a fine sense for
rhythmic continuities in the lines of landscape and figures,
and a delicate precision of detail in the anatomy, brocade and
distant houses. But the rhythms are less artificially forced,
and details are toned down, subordinated to larger masses.
This picture has a spacious freedom in its bold, unsymmetrical design that is more usual in Bouts than in Memling, who
yielded too often to the dead academic conventions of his
time. The landscape background is now almost equal in
importance to the figures, and fairly natural in its irregular
contours. This points the way to Brueghel's later achieve-

FIG. 94. THE MARTYRDOM OF ST. SEBASTIAN
By Memling

ments along that line, and gives the picture an interest lacking in the formal altar-pieces. It was made for a guild of archers.

BOSCH (SCHOOL). THE TEMPTATION OF ST. ANTHONY. (*Fig. 95.*)

Bosch is one of the painters who are creative in the subject-matter they represent, as well as in purely visual qualities of form. He leads one spellbound into a nightmarish fantasy of weird goblins, utterly unreal, and yet so consistent in itself, and so elaborately worked out, as to become a convincing world of its own. It is essentially northern Gothic, not only in subject-matter but in its intricate linear traceries — these goblins' ancestors are to be found in many a cathedral gargoyle and stone relief. But there is always a distinctive touch. He is endlessly inventive in thinking up new monsters and broadly grotesque bodily predicaments. The shock of surprised amusement is constant as one travels through the swarms of them, finding always something previously overlooked. They can scarcely have frightened anyone, for their humorous absurdities are obvious.

The form is consistent, and equally forceful. To organize these numberless details in deep space, without confusion, is a difficult problem, and its successful handling was the inspiration of Pieter Brueghel's equal success in a similar style. Each little figure is drawn with utmost clarity and brief expressiveness — the painter cannot rely on the observer's experience to supply vague details. Each must be contrasted with its neighbors in light or darkness, color and texture, and there is no end to their variety: mottled, shiny, shaggy and scaly; glistening pea-green, scarlet, lemon, fiery orange and delicate tints of rose. Each figure is a pattern in itself, in finely curving, folded-over planes like a

FIG. 95. THE TEMPTATION OF ST. ANTHONY
By Bosch

Gothic wood-carving. And, standing at a little distance, one can see that they are not a disorderly swarm, but marshalled in clear subordinate groupings, festoons that swirl without confusion around the broad, firm basic planes of landscape and architecture.

This picture in Brussels is a well-executed school version of the original in Lisbon. Many of his originals are in the Escorial in Spain, and in poor condition.

Briefer Mention

ROGER VAN DER WEYDEN, *Man with the Arrow* — a strong, simple portrait, with none of the academic tightness of his religious pictures. BRUEGHEL, *Fall of the Rebel Angels; The Census at Bethlehem* — the first shows clearly his derivation from Bosch; the second is Brueghel himself, at his best — scores of little figures in a vividly real snowy village, in apparent disorder, but connected by pervasive rhythms. RUBENS, *The Assumption; The Ascent to Calvary* — subjects congenial to his style, representing swirling upward movement and muscular strain.

BRUGES AND GHENT

The former is notable for its many fine MEMLINGS, especially the *St. Ursula* series (St. John's Hospital); others are in the *Musée Communal*, with two by JAN VAN EYCK: a *Madonna* and a *Portrait of his Wife*. At *Ghent* is the most elaborate and influential of early Flemish works: the *Adoration of the Lamb*, in the church of St. Bavon, by the brothers HUBERT AND JAN VAN EYCK.

The Ryksmuseum

REMBRANDT. THE NIGHT WATCH. (*Fig. 96.*)

This is Rembrandt's most complex and elaborately developed composition. It applies his consummate mastery of light and shade to the task of organizing many figures into a design in deep space. Not often in his later years did that task interest him. Having shown in his youth — in *The Anatomy Lesson* and many of the Biblical etchings — that he could do it with ease, he was often content with single figures, portraits, and fragmentary sketches. Their marvellous finesse in shading, and their haunting psychological expressiveness, are enough as a rule to atone for any lack of pattern; but when that also is provided, the result is a work of monumental power as well as subtlety.

The basic conception, a contrast between long straight lances and the irregular curves of human figures, was not original with Rembrandt. We have seen it in Uccello, and it was used by the ancient Romans in the *Battle of Alexander* mosaic, now at Naples. Nor was the ability to organize many figures in space new with him: it had become common property by the end of the Renaissance. Rembrandt's distinctive contribution was to build up such a design with his own unique materials: his dusky, sombre adaptation of the glowing Venetian atmosphere; his half-lights, containing countless intermediate tones of colored shadow; his drastic simplifications, characteristic of the seventeenth century.

To do the work full justice, we should notice in detail the inventive variation of linear themes in the weapons and costumes; the submerged but graphic expression of individual character (always of vital interest to Rembrandt); the

FIG. 96. THE NIGHT WATCH

By Rembrandt

masterly treatment of surface textures — flesh, steel, wood, wool, silk and stone — not in detail, but with terse rendering of essential differences in lustre. We should follow the pure music of light and color: the sudden climaxes, and the slower, gradual wellings of deep red and greenish gold out of a gloom that is never murky, always pulsating with mysterious tints and shadows. All these are qualities observable to some extent in other works by Rembrandt, however.

So it is wise in this case to return and look long at the way in which he arranges objects in space, with a complexity unsurpassed. There are many easy methods of space composition: converging perspective lines, diminishing the size of distant figures, making nearby figures overlap the farther, and having nearer figures lighter, more distinct, brighter in color. Any of these, when used too obviously and exclusively, gives a mechanical effect, soon tiresome. Rembrandt uses them all at once, with perfect control, lacking only the full use of color-contrasts such as Veronese and Cézanne employ. Light is his chief tool, as always. Far from using it in a crude way — such as making figures lighter and clearer in exact proportion to nearness — he brings in all manner of surprising variations. A face in near, far or middle ground may be brought out in clear emphasis; a hand here, a spear-tip there, is touched by golden light. Let a cloud pass the sun outside the museum window, and they move in and out of the canvas in ghostly animation, but never in confusion. All this in the hands of a lesser man might be mere virtuosity; but here it is so lacking in ostentation, and so well combined with other qualities, as to rest on a firm structure of artistic form.

PIETER DE HOOCH. THE PANTRY. (*Fig. 97.*)

Some of the seventeenth century Dutch, especially Vermeer, de Hooch and Terborch, developed a pleasing and distinctive style in portraying the every-day life of plain people, usually in household or tavern interiors. In form as well as in subject, it represents a reaction away from Renaissance classicism. With the Greek gods and goddesses, the nobles in fine array, there disappeared the suave flourishes of line, the big nude muscles, the grandiloquent gestures, the crimson and gold — all the paraphernalia with which seventeenth century Italian painters were trying to keep alive the dying fire of their national genius. But the basic contributions of Florence and Venice, the principles of deep-space design and richly colored texture, were retained and adapted to a new local subject-matter. In some of the Dutch *genre* school, the interest in amusing incidents and picturesque characters dominates to such an extent that very little artistic form remains (e.g., in Teniers, van Ostade, van Steen). Even de Hooch's work is very uneven in quality; it has often little to offer but skill in representing outdoor sunlight.

The Pantry is a modest, well-balanced combination of design and expressive values. Its associations appeal to the basic human interest in home and family. These are not exaggerated, but quietly made real through the simple, characteristic attitudes and dress of mother and child, and the worn, much lived-in walls of the unpretentious interior. Meanwhile, the picture is satisfying the eye more directly by its harmonious, plain and substantial form. There is a basic contrast of rectangles — in the tiles, doors and windows — with the short, irregular curves of the two persons, the barrel-end, the distant pillow and the face in the portrait. These are arranged in a fairly complex design of

FIG. 97. THE PANTRY
By de Hooch

planes at various angles, and of receding compartments in deep space (Compare the Lippi *Madonna,* Fig. 52). The color-pattern of dark reddish browns and gray-greens is enriched by the softly tinted, deeply realistic textures of wood, stone and cloth. Lights from various sources add soft gradations of shading, and points of climax in the child's gold hair and cap, and the two distant windows.

This type of form had many imitators. Chardin raised it to even higher levels in some of his *genre* pieces, such as *Back from School, Back from Market* and *Grace,* in the Louvre. But in the nineteenth century it sank to low depths of anecdotal banality.

Briefer Mention

JACOB VAN RUYSDAEL, *The Mill* — most famous of Dutch landscapes, expressing the essential qualities of the Dutch countryside: its sober flatness, its cool greens, its towering windmills against cloudy sky. It is typical in its omission of all definite design; but as a rule Jacob, the younger Ruysdael, is given to waterfalls and other wild, tumultuous aspects of nature. VERMEER, *The Little Street; The Letter* — the first is the realistic Vermeer at his best, in plain stone house-walls built of rich, substantial color, full of cloudy, diffused sunlight; the other is a flashy, disorganized attempt at striking pattern.

THE HAGUE

Mauritshuis Gallery

Here the most famous possession is REMBRANDT'S *Anatomy Lesson* — a youthful work, but with his typical interest in dramatic contrast of facial expressions fully developed; the flaring light is also dramatic, but less subtle than in after years. The composition is unusually definite and rhythmic in its design of bearded heads and ruffs, with a foreshortened body pointing to a book that reverses the triangular shape of the group of heads.

VERMEER's *View of Delft* far surpasses all other Dutch landscapes in coloring. It is not in conventional brownish greens, but in his own intense and delicate tints of blue, red and pale yellow, arranged in planes of different hue that organize the scene in space. There is more essential sunlight quality in the distant roofs and reflections on water, than in any other landscape of his school. POTTER's *The Bull* (136) is the sturdy ancestor of a host of cattle-pictures, especially of the Barbizon school.

SALOMON VAN RUYSDAEL. THE BRIDGE. (*Fig. 98; No. 566.*)

This is Dutch landscape at a well-balanced moment of transition between the patterned artificiality of early Flemish work such as Patinir's, and the patternless, photographic naturalism of the later Dutch school (e.g., Jacob van Ruysdael, his nephew). It is inconspicuous, easily overlooked, yet substantial and quietly satisfying. The sharp decorative flourishes are gone, the tiny, detailed, individual leaves and pebbles, and the unnaturally strong color-contrasts between different sections of the ground. But there remains a sense of rhythm and unified design which was afterward sacrificed to the merely realistic and picturesque. Two contrasting themes are unobtrusively interwoven: first the long lines of the boats and bridge, straight or broadly curving, carried out in the broad rolling contours of the land; and, second, a short wavy line that rounds out the blunt silhouettes of the peasants, the tree-trunk and little hillocks, then goes rippling through the branches and the soft, smudged contours of the leafage and the clouds. Strong but not unnatural

FIG. 98. THE BRIDGE
By Salomon van Ruisdael

contrasts of light and shade divide the picture into definite planes and masses, composing it clearly in deep space. The persons, trees and boats are arranged without symmetry but in firm bilateral balance, which accords with the tranquillity of the scene. The color lacks richness and variety: it is largely a monochrome of greenish brown, in washes of different shades and thicknesses. This limitation is to be understood as a phase of the movement toward naturalism, away from unnatural, bright color-patterns. Later painters (Cézanne and Renoir, for example) have been able to combine rich, contrasting color-patterns with a fluent naturalism.

Those aspects of nature and humanity are selected here that express quietness, plainness, snugness, sturdiness, unpretentiousness. We are at a far remove from the other, more Italianate landscape school of the seventeenth century — that of Poussin and Claude Lorrain, with its vast, ordered, park-like expanses, peopled with majestic arching trees, dramatic crags and ruins, and gracefully posed classical personages. With Salomon van Ruysdael and his contemporaries, van Goyen and Cuyp, begins the influential Dutch tradition in landscape. It later inspired Hobbema in Holland, Old Crome and Constable in England, and some of the Barbizon school — Diaz and Rousseau — in France.

HAARLEM

The largest, most elaborate and colorful of the paintings of FRANS HALS are in the local museum: notably his *Group of Arquebusiers*. They express a jovial, swaggering character, or a dignified and masterful one, in appropriate style; but without the subtlety of Rembrandt in either form or expression. There is nothing particularly distinctive in their designs or coloring; and there is more miscellaneous representative detail, less selection of essentials, than in such small sketches as Figure 87.

CHAPTER VII

RUSSIA

TOURIST travel to Russia is not yet large, but is increasing each year, as the outside world discovers its safety and exceptional interest. For that reason this chapter is added as a brief appendix, with no attempt to do more than suggest the high quality of the principal museums there.

The only distinctive Russian school of painting before the revolution, except for peasant arts and crafts, was the making of religious ikons. These were usually Madonnas in the Byzantine style, as a result of the relation of the Russian church to Byzantium or Constantinople. The center of their manufacture was at Kieff, where there is still a notable collection, remarkable for their varied and striking developments of a form long obsolete in western Europe.

The Hermitage Museum of the Czars at St. Petersburg, now Leningrad, was however one of the greatest general collections in the world; and since the revolution it has been further enriched by the nationalized private collections of noblemen all through the country. Much inferior bric-à-brac has been sold, but the best paintings have been kept. At Moscow is one of the two or three outstanding collections of recent impressionist and post-impressionist painting; it far surpasses anything of the sort in western Europe. This is the one formed by Stchoukine and Morosoff, now the public

Museum of Modern Art. A typical example from this, and one from the Hermitage, are reproduced and discussed below.

The Hermitage Museum

To recount the strong features of this museum is to list nearly all the chief national schools of painting from the Renaissance through the eighteenth century. Of all the individual painters, REMBRANDT is best represented, with a panoramic survey of his great portraits and Biblical scenes from youth to old age. After the Dutch, the Venetians and eighteenth century French come next. A late Venetian work is selected for illustration:

PAOLO VERONESE. THE FINDING OF MOSES. (*Fig. 99.*)

In Veronese the Renaissance is at its final culmination, and on the verge of decadence. Its early simplicity and fire are gone: the subjects which inspired it, religious and classical, have lost their novelty and vital importance. The technical problems of three centuries have been solved: Veronese is the complete virtuoso in paint. He has little to say that has not been said by Titian or Tintoretto; but he repeats the glorious Venetian color-forms with an ease and fullness in which there is no slackening of power, so that his works are in many ways as good to look upon as theirs.

From the viewpoint of subject-matter, his great offense in the eyes of serious contemporaries was irreverence, in portraying religious figures with modern clothing, and well-fed, worldly faces, in scenes of merriment. Here that blasé disregard of sacred history, and of chronological realism, is shown in the quite Venetian character of the scene —

FIG. 99. THE FINDING OF MOSES
By Veronese

costumes, dwarf, negro slave, and the rest. Such liberties involve some inconsistency between the form and the ordinary associations of the subject. But they are to some extent a virtue rather than a fault in modern eyes, since they allow unlimited freedom to develop the form by purely visual standards.

Other qualities that mark the picture as Veronese's are, first of all, the emphasis on surface texture. The brocaded dress of the lady, in particular, has a gorgeous metallic lustre of bright gold over white satin, that focusses all the whites of sky and clothing, and the greenish golds of hair and leaves. A second, and even more distinctive trait, is the importance of cool silver-grays and pale blues in the color scheme, offsetting the gold and brown. Red, so dominant as a rule in Titian and Tintoretto, is reduced to a few pale streaks of rose in subordinate places. A third is the gentle, swirling flow of movement, less vigorous than in Tintoretto. Finally, there is the distinctive skill, which Veronese shows in most of his large group pictures, in using contrasting colors to make certain figures advance or recede, and thus to arrange them in space. The gold-brocaded dress, the yellow shirt of the negro, and the golden leaves, all tend to advance from their contexts; the blue and pale violet costumes in between, and the silver-blue distant landscape, all recede. This effect, of course, is related to light, scale and perspective, to give each object its exact position in space.

Briefer Mention

These representative titles will suggest the broad scope of the collection.

Italian. BOTTICELLI, *Adoration of the Magi.* PERUGINO, *Crucifixion, with the Virgin and Saints.* RAPHAEL, *St. George.* LEONARDO DA VINCI, *The Litta Madonna.*

CORREGGIO, *Madonna of the Milk*. GIORGIONE, *Judith*. TITIAN, *The Toilet of Venus; Danaë*. TINTORETTO, *Birth of St. John the Baptist*. CARAVAGGIO, *Mandolin-player*.

Spanish. EL GRECO, *Sts. Peter and Paul*. VELAZQUEZ, *Portrait of the Count of Olivares*. ZURBARAN, *St. Laurence*.

Flemish and Dutch. JAN VAN EYCK, *The Last Judgment*. ROGER VAN DER WEYDEN, *St. Luke Drawing the Virgin's Portrait*. BOUTS, *Annunciation*. HALS, *Portrait of a Man*. REMBRANDT, *Danaë; The Return of the Prodigal Son*. DE HOOCH, *Lady and Cook*. JACOB VAN RUYSDAEL, *Swamp Landscape*. TERBORCH, *A Glass of Lemonade*. POTTER, *Departure for the Hunt*. CUYP, *Landscape with Cows*. RUBENS, *Bacchanale*.

German and French. CRANACH, *The Virgin in the Arbor*. CLOUET, *The Duke of Alençon*. POUSSIN, *Historical Landscape*. CLAUDE LORRAIN, *Morning; Noon; Evening; Night*. WATTEAU, *The Hardships of War*. LANCRET, *Spring; Summer*. CHARDIN, *The Laundress*.

MOSCOW

The Modern Art Museum

All too little has been said of contemporary, post-impressionist art in this book, for the reason that little of it has yet found a place in public galleries. Museum authorities are notoriously slow in recognizing the significant movements of their own generations. The public museums of the world are just beginning, through private bequests and hesitant costly purchases, to exhibit some of the impressionist pictures which were radical in the seventies. Still more rarely, examples are coming to be seen here and there of the early post-impressionist movement of the end of the nineteenth century.

The Moscow Museum of Modern Art is unique in Europe as a public gallery devoted entirely to the advanced, experimental movements of the last three generations. Its contents were assembled before the revolution, it is true, and by a nobleman and a wealthy industrialist, not a proletarian. But the present government has been wise enough to conserve them for public use. Only one or two private collections of modern art in the world approach this one in importance.

All the chief controversial figures of the last half of the nineteenth century are here. COURBET is represented by a *Landscape* blocked in heavily with palette-knife, its broad converging planes of roofs and mountain peaks anticipating Cézanne. MANET has another sketch, *Man with a Pipe*. The younger impressionists are better represented: MONET with a large early work, *The Picnic*, somewhat in the style of Manet, and with several later pictures in soft, shimmering broken color, notably *Boulevard des Capucines* and *Gardencorner at Montgeron*. Works of SISLEY, PISSARRO, and of RENOIR and CÉZANNE in their impressionist period, round out the exhibit of that generation.

CÉZANNE's later, solid style is splendidly represented by several *Still-life* groups comparable to the one in Munich (Fig. 80); by several portraits, including one of himself and one of *Madame Cézanne;* and by some powerful landscapes, including one of *Mont St. Victoire.* There is no important late example of RENOIR, but there are several of his most delightful nudes and portraits of the seventies and eighties, especially a *Bather* of 1878. DEGAS is shown in all his mature phases: a light, dainty *Dancer at the Photographer's*, a heavy pastel of dancers *In the Wings*, and a bizarrely naturalistic, richly colored *After the Bath*.

Among the younger post-impressionists of that day, GAUGUIN is best represented, with over a score of his largest, most elaborate canvases of the Tahiti period. One of these is therefore chosen for illustration and discussion here.

GAUGUIN. WOMAN WITH A PIECE OF FRUIT. (*Fig. 100.*)

Like many of his contemporaries, Gauguin began as an impressionist in France, then went on to another aim and technique in his later work. Where Cézanne emphasized solidity, Gauguin emphasized flat, decorative pattern, with broad areas of bright, plain, contrasting color, enclosed by lines of primitive, blunt simplicity. It is a striking form, but weaker and cruder than those of Cézanne and Renoir, and a good share of its success has been due to the romantic associations of its South Sea Island subjects and the painter's life there.

The picture shown is typical of Gauguin's charm and limitations. There is impressionist feeling for sunlight in the intense, tropical yellow of the background, clouded with fantastic shadows of a greenish gold scarcely less hot. But there is no sparkle or genuine realism; sunlight and shadow are transformed into decorative contrasts on a flat screen. Against it the woman's body is another flat section, in which the sun's gold sinks to golden brown. In her dress the leaves' bright green becomes paler, and the pink fruit she holds is a repetition of others on the tree and on the ground. There is a flow of curves in the background, with bent verticals against it. The crude vigor of such a scheme, borrowed from primitive painting and textiles, was refreshing in an age still hardly aware of any but the main European tradition in art. But after its first refreshing shock has passed, one looks in vain for inner subtleties to hold the attention.

FIG. 100. WOMAN WITH A PIECE OF FRUIT
By Gauguin

Of the same group, VAN GOGH has contributed several typically agitated, bright-colored portraits and landscapes, and HENRI ROUSSEAU ("le douanier") one of his jungle scenes of clear-cut, deeply interlacing tropical leaves: *The Horse and the Tiger*.

Among the men of the present generation, MATISSE and PICASSO, the two dominating figures, are both extensively represented. In particular, Matisse has a brightly flowered *Red Room*, with vivid opposition of crude cherry-red, gray-blue, lemon and emerald — his own new harmonies, full of clashing dissonance. Picasso is shown in several of his different periods: an early, Greco-like, emaciated *Old Jew and Boy*, in blue; and several cubist portraits, still-life groups and landscapes, among them the much-reproduced *Factories at La Huerta*. DERAIN, BRACQUE, ROUAULT, VLAMINCK and a few others of the present day complete the list, as they do at the *Luxembourg* in Paris — each striking out on a different path, whose outcome is yet to be disclosed.

INDEX OF PAINTERS, WITH DATES

Numbers in italics indicate analyses of pictures illustrated

Albertinelli (1474–1515), 79.

Altdorfer (1480–1538), 213.

Angelico, Fra (1387–1455), xxxv, 79, *159.*

Apelles (4th cent. B.C.), xxxiii, 107.

Avignon, School of, 80.

Basaiti (1470–1530), *175.*

Bellini, Gentile (1429–1507), 174.

Bellini, Giovanni (1428–1516), xxxv, 16, *140,* 169, 178.

Böcklin (1827–1900), 235.

Boel (1625–78), 220.

Blake (1757–1827), xxxvi, 21, *23,* 25.

Bonington (1802–28), 21.

Bosch (1460–1516), xxxv, 101, 103, *264.*

Botticelli (1444–1510), xxxv, 79, 120, *137,* 190, 279.

Boucher (1703–70), xxxvi, *63,* 223.

Bouts (1410–75), xxxv, 223, *260,* 280.

Bracque (contemporary), 82, 284.

Brouwer (1605–38), 101, 223.

Brueghel (1525–69), xxxv, 101, *193, 215,* 259, 266.

Burne-Jones (1833–98), 21.

Byzantine School, *152, 154, 186,* 189, 276.

Canaletto (1697–1768), 178, 234.

Caravaggio (1569–1609), 146, 280.

Carpaccio (1460–1522), xxxv, 79, *172.*

Castagno, A. dal (1410–57), 16, 163.

Cavallini (13th cent.), 130.

Cézanne (1839–1906), xxxvi, 21, 81, *226,* 256, 281.

Chardin (1699–1779), xxxvi, *64,* 211, 223, 280.

Chinese, xxx, 25, *27, 29,* 81, 85, 256.

Chirico (contemporary), xxxvii.

Cimabue (1240?–1301?), 145.

Clouet, François (1510–72), 80, 280.

Constable (1776–1837), xxxvi, *11,* 21, 40, 212, 256.

Corot (1796–1875), xxxvi, 81.

Correggio (1494–1534), 101, 130, 189, *252*, 280.

Courbet (1819–77), xxxvi, 81, 212, *235*, 256, 281.

Cranach (1472–1553), 101, 213, *240*, 280.

Cristus, Petrus (1410–72), *240*.

Crivelli (1430?–1493?), 9.

Crome (1768–1821), 17.

Cuyp (1620–91), 280.

Daumier (1810–79), 21, 81, 212, 256.

David, Gerard (1464–1523), 259.

David, J. L. (1748–1825), xxxvi, 67.

Degas (1834–1917), xxxvii, *76*, 78, 281.

Delacroix (1798–1863), xxxvi, *69*, 85, 212, 256.

Derain (contemporary), xxxvii, 82, 284.

Duccio (1260–1339), xxxv, *134*.

Dürer (1471–1528), 80, 101, 202, *206*, *208*, 212, 238.

Dyck, Van (1599–1641), 202, 211.

Egyptian, xxxiii, *25*.

Eyck, Hubert Van (1366–1426), xxxv, 266.

Eyck, Jan Van (1385?–1441), xxxv, 7, 79, 234, 266, 280.

Flandes, Juan de (15th–16th cent.), 202.

Fouquet (1415–80), xxxv, 80.

Fragonard (1732–1806), xxxvi, *19*, 80.

Francesca, Piero della (1416?–92), xxxv, 16, *131*.

Froment (active 1461–82), 80.

Gainsborough (1727–88), 21.

Gauguin (1848–1903), xxxvii, 21, 82, 235, *282*.

Ghirlandaio, Domenico (1449–94), 163.

Giorgione (1477–1510), xxxv, *47*, 146, 170, 189, 202, *231*, 280.

Giotto (1266–1337), xxxv, 131, 145, *163*, *166*.

Gogh, Van (1853–90), xxxvii, 21, *229*, 235, 284.

Goya (1746–1828), xxxvi, *95*, 97, 256.

Goyen, Van (1596–1656), xxxv.

Gozzoli, Benozzo (1420–98), *161*.

Greco, El (1548–1625), xxxv, 9, 79, *93*, 99, 102, 103, 280.

Greek, xxxiii, 25, 107.

Grünewald (active 1480–1530), 192, *213*, *215*.

Guardi (1712–93), 178.

Hals (1580?–1666), xxxv, 17, 79, *244*, 275.

Hiroshige (1797–1858), xxxiv, 82.

Hobbema (1638–1709), 13, 16.

Hogarth (1697–1764), 17.

Hokusai (1760–1849), xxxiv, *31*, 82.

Holbein (1497–1543), 17, 80, *197*, 234, 238.

Hooch, P. de (1629–77), 17, *270*.

Indian, xxx, 25, *38*, 40, 81.

Ingres (1780–1867), xxxvi, *67*.

Japanese, xxxiv, 25, *31*, *33*, 81, 85, 256.

Jordaens (1593–1678), *195*, 220.

Klee (contemporary), 256.

Kokoschka (contemporary), 256.

Korin (d. 1716), xxxiv.

Ku K'ai Chih (4th–5th cent.), xxxiv, 25.

Lancret (1690–1743), 81, 234.

Le Nain, Louis (17th cent.), xxxv, 80.

Leyden, Lucas Van (1494–1533), 212.

Li Lung Mien (11th–12th cent.), xxxiv.

Limbourg, Pol de (15th cent.), 86.

Lippi, Filippo (1406?–69), xxxv, 145, *149*, 151, 161, 254.

Lochner (d. 1451), xxxv, 191.

Longhi (1702–85), 178.

Lorenzetti, Ambrogio (active 1323–48), 134.

Lorenzetti, Pietro (active 1306–48), 133, 134.

Lorenzo Monaco (1370?–1425), 114, 139, 152.

Lorrain, Claude (1600–82), xxxv, *58*, 101, 223, 280.

Lotto, Lorenzo (1480–1556), *54*, 101.

Manet (1832–83), xxxvi, 21, 81, 85, *224*, 256, 281.

Mantegna (1431–1506), xxxv, *52*, 146, 170, 178.

Marc (contemporary), 256.

Martini, Simone (1283–1344), 78, 133, 145.

Masaccio (1401–28), *156*.

Massys, Quentin (1466–1530), 259.

Master from Delft (15th cent.), 9.

Master of Georgslegende (active 1460), 192.

Master of the Holy Kinship (early 16th cent.), 192.

Master of the Lyversberg Passion (active 1460–80), 192.

Master of the Pearl of Brabant (15th cent.), 223.

Matabei (16th–17th cent.), 25.

Matisse (1869–), xxxvii, *83*, 284.

Ma Yuan (12th–13th cent.), xxxiv.

Medieval, xxxiii, 24, 85, 113, 130, *152*, *154*, 163, *186*, 190, 211.

Memling (1430–94), xxxv, 262, 266.

Memmi, Lippo (d. 1352), 145.

Michelangelo (1475–1564), xxxv, 120.

Monet (1840–1926), xxxvi, 71, 82, 212, 235, 281.

Mu Ch'i (10th cent.), 27.

Murillo (1617–82), 87, 101.

Orcagna (1308?–68), 152, 163.

Patinir (1480–1524), 101, 242.

Persian, xxx, 25, 35, 81.

Perugino (1446–1523), 79, 120, 279.

Picasso (1881–   ), xxxvii, 284.

Pietro, Sano di (1406–81), 134.

Pinturicchio (1454–1513), 134.

Pisanello (1397?–1455), 16, 79.

Pissarro (1831–1903), xxxvi, 212, 281.

Pollaiuolo, A. del (1432–98), 143.

Potter (1625–54), 203, 273, 280.

Poussin (1594–1665), xxxv, 54, 101, 223, 234, 280.

Prehistoric, xxxii, 86.

Puvis de Chavannes, Pierre (1824–98), 85, 235.

Raphael (1483–1520), xxxv, 50, 126, 129, 146, 147, 190, 231, 279.

Rembrandt (1606–69), xxxv, 17, 25, 40, 50, 80, 208, 234, 246, 267, 272, 280.

Renoir (1841–1919), xxxvi, 21, 73, 82, 212, 256, 281.

Reynolds (1723–92), 21.

Ribera (1588–1656), 101.

Roman, xxix, 105, 107, 108, 110, 114, 116, 130.

Romney (1734–1802), 21.

Rossetti (1828–82), 21.

Rouault (contemporary), 82, 284.

Rousseau, Henri (1844–1910), xxxvii, 284.

Rubens (1577–1640), xxxv, 13, 17, 79, 101, 199, 201, 211, 217, 234, 260, 266, 280.

Ruysdael, Jacob Van (1629–81), xxxv, 234, 272, 280.

Ruysdael, Salomon Van (1600–70), xxxv, 273, 275.

Sargent (1856–1925), 21.

Sarto, A. del (1486–1531), 146.

Segonzac, A. de (contemporary), 82.

Sesshu (1420–1506), xxxiv, 25.

Seurat (1859–91), xxxvi, 21, 82.

Signac (contemporary), 82.

Signorelli (1441–1523), 131, 254.

Sisley (1839–99), xxxvi, 82, 281.

Sotades (5th cent. B.C.), 25.

Strigel (1461–1528), 212, 213.

Terborch (1617–81), 202, 254, 280.

Tiepolo (1696–1769), 16.

Tintoretto (1518–94), xxxv, 6, 16, 50, 78, 101, 146, 170, 177, *178*, *181*, 183, 190, 280.

Titian (1477–1576), xxxv, *4*, *50*, 78, 101, 130, 146, 169, *170*, 202, 223, *249*, 280.

Toulouse-Lautrec (1864–1901), 82, 235.

Tura, Cosimo (1420–95), 79.

Turner (1775–1851), xxxvi, *14*, 21.

Uccello (1397–1475), xxxv, *2*.

Utamaro (d. 1788), xxxiv, *33*.

Utrillo (contemporary), 82.

Velazquez (1599–1660), xxxv, 17, 19, 79, *90*, *91*, 100, 103, 130, 202, 280.

Veneziano, Domenico (active 1438–61), 145, *254*.

Vermeer (1632–75), xxxv, 80, *203*, 234, *254*, 272.

Veronese, Paolo (1528–88), xxxv, 7, 78, 101, 170, 177, *184*, 277.

Verrocchio (1435–88), 145.

Vinci, Leonardo da (1452–1519), xxxv, *44*, 145, 190, 279.

Vivarini, Alvise (1447–1504), 178.

Vlaminck (contemporary), 82, 284.

Watteau (1683–1721), xxxvi, 19, *60*, 234, 280.

Watts (1817–1904), 21.

Weyden, Roger Van der (1400–64), xxxv, 103, *257*, 266.

Whistler (1834–1903), *21*.

Witz, Konrat (early 15th cent.), 256.

Zeuxis (5th cent. B.C.), xxxiii, 107.

Zurbaran (1598–1662), 101, 280.

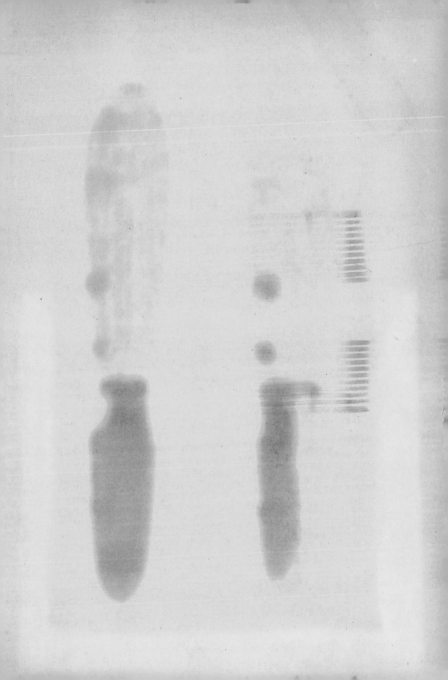

DATE DUE

GAYLORD   PRINTED IN U.S.A.